SCARED SITLESS

SCARED SITLESS

The Office Fitness Book

LARRY SWANSON

Foreword
Joan Vernikos, PhD

ISBN-13: 978-0-9912441-3-3
ISBN-10: 0-9912441-3-3

Elless Media, LLC
Seattle, WA
www.ellessmedia.com

Ordering Information:

Quantity sales. Special discounts are available on quantity purchases by corporations, associations, and others. For details, contact the publisher at the web address above.

Orders by U.S. trade bookstores and wholesalers. Please contact Ingram: phone 800-937-8000 or visit www.ingramcontent.com

This information in this book is intended only to offer general information on the topics of office fitness and workplace health. Although every effort has been made to review and present only reliable and safe information, some material may not be appropriate for every reader. Your age, health, fitness level, and other factors all affect your ability to safely use this or any health and fitness information. If you have any doubts about your ability to safely implement any of the information here, consult your doctor.

Dedicated to all office workers everywhere,
but especially to Mom, who refuses to retire.

Contents

Foreword

The development of new concepts and ways of approaching a commonplace subject in a novel way usually come from individuals who are not one-dimensional in thought. Most are curious about everything around them, about how to do, solve or design something to find ways of improving their area of expertise. Larry Swanson first called me up three years ago after coming across my book Sitting Kills, Moving Heals. We were on the same wavelength. It was easy to share views on what would seem a counterintuitive concept to others. Having to regularly help "wounded office-warriors" as patients in pain on his massage table, Larry spontaneously identified commonalities between our ways of thinking. *Scared Sitless* is the distillation of these thoughts and experience. Larry brings his extensive knowledge of the human body and personal experience as an office worker to understanding and correcting the myriad adverse consequences of sitting.

So what is wrong with sitting? We all do it. We have to sit. Yet modern life has driven us to sitting for most of our waking hours. The chair, invented as a means to transport people, has now become a crutch and a disservice to human health. Sitting in a chair came to replace the natural stance of squatting, depriving us of functional strength and maintenance of body parts crucial to our independence. Squatting enables up and down motion with naturally correct body posture that sitting in a chair, not to mention a cushy padded chair, eliminates. Studies of the ills of prolonged sitting have mushroomed in the last three years. Yet office work that for most of us takes up a good part of the day has barely been touched. Larry tackles this vacuum in his book. He does this effectively, comprehensively, and with humor. The bibliographic information is thorough.

Office work has not always meant being glued to a screen sitting at a desk. Dickensian clerks stood or leaned on a tall stool all day. Some enlightened office managers then recognized the problem and tried to do something about it. I met Ann Martin, an elegant centenarian, at one of my talks in Colorado. She was a steno-typist, if anyone knows what that is, who in the 70s worked for Met Life in their HQ building on New York's Fifth Avenue where the policy was for all to get out of their chairs at 11am and 3pm walk to an open window, breathe deeply and stretch arms above the head before returning to their seats. On asking how long she sat for in between these mandatory breaks she was surprised; she was called several times a day to go into her boss's office for dictation. How things have changed. Met Life now no longer adheres to this policy and their windows are fixed closed.

Larry Swanson reviews the relative merits of different available solutions and puts forward his own ideas to keep you happy at work and away from the masseur or orthopedic surgeon. Upright desks, ergonomically designed chairs, PCs, or keyboards have been flooding the market and he suggests sensible and practical guidance to these choices. Particularly useful are the tips that people can apply for quick relief. Discussion on self-awareness, posture, and how we can change habits will be useful to everyone because they do not only apply to sitting.

As a firm advocate of breaking up sitting by standing often, I began counting how many times I came across the phrase "take a break." I quit counting after 20. You will keep coming back to this excellent reference book that is tinged with humor and common sense.

Joan Vernikos PhD
Former Director of NASA Life Sciences

Prologue

It's an exciting time in the world of office fitness. More and more people are standing and walking at their desk jobs. New research is published almost every day about the hazards of sitting and, more importantly, what you can do about them. Furniture manufacturers are cranking out an impressive array of adjustable-height desks, and gadgets are appearing to measure how much you move and to monitor your posture at work. In the fall of 2013, the world's first treadmill desk and standing desk store opened in Seattle. My goal in this book is to share my excitement about these developments with you and to give you practical, actionable ideas about how to implement them.

I make three pretty big claims on the cover of this book: that you can work happier, lose weight, and live longer by applying what you learn here about office fitness (first lesson, please stand up as you read this prologue; I'll explain why when you get to the end).

Can better office fitness habits actually help you **work happier**? If your happiness at work is elevated by reducing the amount of pain that you experience day to day, by improving your vitality, and by helping you become more productive and effective at work, then, yes, I can confidently state that better office fitness habits will help you work happier. I'll set out abundant evidence showing how better physical fitness habits can reduce the amount of pain you experience. I'll show how incorporating even just a little more routine movement into your workday can boost your vigor and vitality. I'll share research findings that show how improving your posture can not only change how you feel in your body but also change how others perceive you, giving you more authority and influence at work.

Can better office fitness habits actually help you **lose weight**? Absolutely. The core thesis of this book is that we need to be more routinely active at work. Many of the key habits that I hope you'll adopt revolve around this idea. The more you move, the more calories you'll burn. The more calories you burn, the less you'll weigh. It's basic physics (nicely set out in a book by sedentary-studies pioneer James Levine, "Move a Little, Lose a Lot"). Not that losing weight in and of itself is the be-all and end-all of any fitness program. Many fit people appear to be overweight, and many trim-looking people couldn't fight their way out of a wet paper bag. Fitness should always trump weight loss in your overall health plan. Still, weight loss is a legitimate concern for lots of people, and better office fitness habits can help you shed a few pounds.

Can better office fitness habits actually help you **live longer**? If you accept the reams of evidence about how deadly it is to sit all day, then, yes. Reversing your lethal sedentary work style by becoming more routinely active at work can only increase your lifespan. One of the earliest research studies on sedentary behavior demonstrated that trolley drivers, who sat all day, were at twice the risk for heart disease as trolley conductors, who stood most of the day. More recent studies bolster the claim that simply standing for even part of the day can reduce your risk of serious disease. Even fidgeting and other seemingly insignificant movements appear to help fend off the dangerous physiological effects of sedentariness. With the introduction of treadmill desks and similar innovations you can even move while you do your desk work.

Which leads to the central idea in this book. **We must become more routinely active at work.** The sedentary nature of modern office work is, quite literally, killing us. Simply standing up for the 5 minutes or so that it takes you to read this prologue triggers mechanisms in your body that help to regulate your blood pressure, re-engage your "second heart" (deep muscles in your calves that help pump blood back up to your heart), trigger the release of enzymes that help to optimize your cholesterol levels, and reactivate a number of other vital physiological functions that are shut off as soon as you sit down. Taking a few steps, even just walking in place, activates even more beneficial physiological mechanisms. At this time, there is much more evidence of the harm caused by sedentary behavior than of the benefits of not being sedentary. It is a reasonable (and testable) hypothesis that restoring more routine movement throughout our workdays will reduce our risk of disease and early death from sedentariness. Because incorporating more routine movement into your office workday is so important, helping you to do that is the main goal of this book.

My work as a massage therapist in downtown Seattle introduced me to other problems caused by office work, and I offer some solutions for those as well. This book arose from being surrounded by the offices of Amazon, Nordstrom, The Gates Foundation, and other companies large and small. My work with their office workers over the past 15 years showed me the results of repetitive, demanding work in stressful environments. Workstations that aren't always ergonomically optimized cause or exacerbate ailments ranging from headaches to low-back pain, from "mouse shoulder" to carpal tunnel syndrome, from mild anxiety to jaw clenching and teeth grinding, from insomnia to fibromyalgia and dozens of other maladies that cause discomfort and pain. Cultivating better habits in the areas of ergonomic self-assessment, posture and body awareness, and at-work and for-work exercise has helped my clients deal with these problems.

Conveniently enough, routine movement can also alleviate many of the musculoskeletal problems I see in my massage practice. As one of my massage teachers says, "Motion is lotion." The more you move, the better your body works. So whether you are concerned with reducing the amount of pain you experience day to day or with reducing your risk of serious long-term health problems, moving more at work is the right solution. My goal in this book is to help you achieve this goal. Please let me know how I'm doing. You can reach me at larry@sitless.com.

Introduction
A New Conception of Fitness

Something's not right here. Western culture is obsessed with fitness, yet we become less fit, more obese, and sicker every year. Experts predict that the current generation will be the first to live shorter lives than their parents.

What's going on?

We are certainly eating differently than we did 40 or 50 years ago, guzzling down sugar and processed foods like there's no tomorrow. We arguably lead more stressful lives than our parents. We don't get enough sleep.

But the blame also lies in our sedentary lifestyles. Vast bodies of research have shown that our lack of regular physical activity is slowly killing us. Addressing this problem by restoring more routine activity to our lives, in particular our office work lives, is the main goal of this book.

Physical inactivity is a problem throughout our culture. Children play video games instead of outdoor games. Instead of running or riding their bikes through the neighborhood to play with friends or go to school they are shuttled everywhere in minivans. When they do get to school, they sit all day, recess time and physical fitness classes having been crowded out by ostensibly more important educational activities. Grown ups drive home from work and plop down in front of the television or computer or game console. Instead of actually visiting friends, we "friend" or "follow" them on our computers. When we do visit, we drive everywhere. It seems that every physical activity we used to do ourselves (opening the garage door, raking leaves, etc.) now has a gadget to do it for us. We are moving less and less throughout our lives.

It's not that we are bad, lazy people. I'm convinced that most of us are truly doing our best to take care of ourselves. I blame the convergence of a hundred years of labor-saving devices (elevators, cars with power steering and power door locks, garage-door openers, computers, leaf blowers, electric can openers, wheeled suitcases, etc.) as well as seismic shifts in the economy that have taken most workers out of farms and factories and put us in offices. Fewer and fewer opportunities to do even minor physical movement combined with stationary, sedentary, stressful, repetitive, indoor office work have lead to these big changes in our physical fitness and health levels. We've just been a bit slow to adapt to these changes. Now that we have the information that we need about how deadly inactivity is, we can act to restore routine physical movement into our workday.

If inactivity is a problem everywhere, why does this book focus only on the office? Two reasons. First, office work is what I know. The ideas that spawned this book originated with my massage practice in downtown Seattle. After 15 years of working with computer programmers, attorneys, designers, sales people, and other office-bound professionals I had identified a number of predictable patterns of pain and postural distortion that come with office work. Also, prior to my massage career I had worked in offices myself for more than a dozen years, and I continue to do a lot of writing and publishing and other desk work, so I have a personal stake in the issue.

Second, the majority of employment in the modern western world now revolves around the office, putting nearly 100 million Americans, for example, into desk jobs. Compounding the issue, the ever-increasing automation of office work makes it less physical every year. You don't have to be much over 40 to recall when office work was at least a bit more physical, back when you had to flip through ledgers of actual spreadsheets, stand up and open filing cabinet drawers, and pack a physical document into a padded envelope and walk it down to the mailroom. Even if you're not a desk worker per se, your job likely involves some computer time to write reports, research technical information, or learn new skills. And no matter what you do for a living, your job has likely been automated to one extent or another to make it less physically demanding.

As I embarked on this project, I had an "aha!" moment when I learned that the research consistently shows that we can't simply exercise our way out of this problem. Numerous studies have now demonstrated that we face the risks of our sedentary lifestyles are regardless of how much we exercise. You could run a 10K every night after work and a marathon every weekend and still be at risk if you sat at a desk eight hours a day during the week. Even if you're among the small percentage of people who are actually working out regularly, even if you are as fit as a fiddle, even if you look like a Greek god or goddess, you are still at the same risk for disease as your less-fit colleagues. In the language of science, sedentary behavior is an "independent risk factor," one you face every time you sit down at your desk, regardless of your outside-the-office fitness level.

Even if you could exercise your way out of the problem, you probably wouldn't. You have no doubt seen the government recommendation for physical activity — 30 minutes of moderate to vigorous exercise at least five times per week. There is good science behind this recommendation, and we should all be striving to reach it. So, how many people do you think actually achieve this goal? Based on the amount of workout gear and gym memberships sold, you might guess it was in the neighborhood of 30%. Indeed, that is about how many people reported achieving the 30-times-5 goal when Judy Kruger and her colleagues at the Centers for Disease Control asked people about their exercise habits. But when you attach accelerometers to people and measure their actual duration of exercise, Richard Troiano and his colleagues at the National Cancer Institute found that fewer than 5% are actually doing that much activity. That's a pretty big discrepancy (which I now think about every time I see someone in the gym leaning on a weight machine between sets, strolling to the pull-up bar, or sipping water by an elliptical trainer. "Hey," I imagine them saying to themselves, "I'm in the gym, so this time counts, right?").

More to the point, think about how little time 30 minutes is compared to a 24-hour day. Here's the math. Even if you are among the 5% of people who actually exercise 150 minutes per week, your exercise time averages out to about 22 minutes per day over a seven-day week. Those 22 minutes are less than 2% of the 1,440 minutes in each day. Compare this with the 400 or more minutes per day you likely spend at your desk, the 400 minutes or so that you sleep, the 60 minutes you spend in the car, the hour or two sitting in front of the TV, and the hour or so you spend sitting down for meals and you begin to see the problem.

This math matters because there's a huge qualitative difference between sedentary time and activity time. When you are sedentary, a whole array of crucial biological functions simply shuts down (much more on this in Chapter 1). When you are at all active — even simply standing as opposed to sitting — those functions come back to life.

The harm that sitting inflicts on you accrues regardless of what you're doing the rest of the time, so it behooves you to figure out how to sit less and to move more during the day. Assuming that you're stuck with your commute, that you'll still sit down to take meals, and that you'll still relax with some TV or computer time after work, this leaves your workday as the best opportunity to become more routinely active.

Restoring routine movement to your workday will add years to your life, but you also need to move right. Moving properly — conducting your office work in a supportive ergonomic environment with good posture and doing exercises that address the unique physical challenges of office work — can prevent the painful neck, shoulder, arm, back, and other ailments that afflict so many office workers. So the scope of this book also includes chapters on how to monitor and maintain your ergonomic set-up, how to develop more body self-awareness and better posture, and how to develop exercise regimens that specifically address the challenges of a desk job.

Physical fitness is typically defined by doctors, exercise physiologists, and personal trainers as a measure of your strength, flexibility, aerobic capacity, body composition (fat vs. muscle vs. bone), and ability to balance. These are important measures, and I encourage you to undertake a fitness program to improve them all.

This book focuses on helping you get more routinely active at work, but, please, don't think that this alone will keep you fit. There is a huge amount of evidence that achieving that 30-minutes of exercise five days a week goal will add years to your life and quality to those years, so keep up your gym membership and fitness routines.

But, as I have hinted at above and as you'll see later in this book, there is also a baseline level of metabolic and cardiovascular fitness that underlies these traditional measures of fitness. You can improve this level of fitness simply by getting up out of your chair and moving on a regular basis. There is also a baseline level of musculoskeletal fitness that you can achieve with exertion levels lower than those of typical athletically biased training programs.

We don't all have to be athletes to be fit.

We need a new conception of fitness that accounts for these basic levels of fitness, one that helps us achieve a foundation for our day-to-day health (as well as for our more ambitious and specific athletic and fitness goals). This idea of fitness should be realistic and achievable for anyone, even people not disposed to regular gym attendance, even people stuck in a chair for most of the day. This new conception of fitness should fit naturally into our work and home lives.

Hundreds of people much smarter than I are working on this problem (and you'll see their names throughout this book as I cite their research). Working in areas such as exercise physiology, obesity studies, inactivity physiology, oncology, and public health, these expert researchers have shown, and continue to show, us the problems associated with prolonged sedentary behavior. Almost every one of their research reports concludes with a sentence like this: "Given these hazards of sedentary behavior, it makes sense to get up and move on a regular basis." To this point, though, they can't offer definitive scientifically vetted recommendations on exactly what we should be doing. There simply isn't much research yet that shows the efficacy of specific amounts of low-level physical activity in reversing the problems of sedentariness. Still, virtually all of these well-informed experts are convinced that we need to be moving more, so anything we can do to re-incorporate routine physical activity into our lives is certain to help.

So far none of these experts has focused on holistically addressing the fitness needs of office workers. That's my modest attempt here, to show you how to keep fit while staying productively employed in your office job. I call this "office fitness." You can call it whatever you'd like, but, please, stand up and walk around as you talk about it.

Sources

"2008 Physical Activity Guidelines for Americans." Health.gov (U.S. Office of Disease Prevention and Health Promotion).

Kruger, Judy, Michelle M. Yore, and Harold W. Kohl. "Leisure-Time Physical Activity Patterns by Weight Control Status: 1999-2002

NHANES." Medicine & Science in Sports & Exercise 39, no. 5 (May 2007): 788–95.

Troiano, Richard P., David Berrigan, Kevin W. Dodd, Louise C. MâSse, Timothy Tilert, and Margaret Mcdowell. "Physical Activity in the United States Measured by Accelerometer:" Medicine & Science in Sports & Exercise 40, no. 1 (January 2008): 181–88.

Chapter 1
Sitting and Other Hazards of Office Work

Our grandparents breathed in coal dust all day, baled hay in the hot sun, and did backbreaking factory work. Now, with the economy shifted from agriculture and industry to services and information, most of us have moved from physically demanding jobs in mining, farming, and manufacturing to comfortable, indoor office jobs. It's tempting to regard that move as progress.

Now we are learning that cushy indoor office work comes at a high cost. Sedentary behavior is, quite literally, killing us. Reams of research show conclusively that sitting all day is deadly. Our immobile desk jobs put us at risk for cancer, diabetes, hypertension, heart disease, obesity, and what health researchers call "all-cause mortality," — the chance that you'll die for any reason. Joseph A. Knight, a scientist at the University of Utah, summarized these risks in a 2012 paper. His study also showed that sedentary behavior puts us at greater risk of osteoporosis, bone fractures, muscle loss, physical disability, depression, dementia, Alzheimer's disease, atherosclerosis, immune system dysfunction, and metabolic syndrome. The British Journal of Sports Medicine says that "physical inactivity is one of the most important public health problems of the 21st century, and may even be the most important." Think about that. Our sedentary ways could be a bigger public health problem than smoking, drinking, gun violence, and any number of infectious diseases.

The scariest detail in these research findings? It doesn't matter how much you exercise after work, how fit you are in general, or how genetically predisposed you are to a long and healthy life. "Sitting is an independent risk factor," says Peter Katzmarzyk, an obesity researcher. No matter how active you are after work, if you sit all day, you will die sooner than you would have otherwise. You'll also suffer more disability for a longer period of time in your final years. End of story.

Yikes! That's some seriously scary news.

So, what's going on? Why are we sitting so much? And how exactly is sitting doing us so much harm?

Why We Sit

We sit because **we all have office jobs** now. Well, not all of us, but certainly a lot more than 60 or 80 years ago. Back then, many more of us worked in mining, farming, or manufacturing. Automation in those industries, along with other big changes in the economy have taken most of us out of farms and factories and put us into service jobs, many of which involving sitting at a desk all day.

We sit because **that's the way offices have been organized**, and mostly still are. Desks are a great place to put typewriters, piles of paper, staplers, telephones, and the other accouterments of traditional office work, and chairs are a great way to situate yourself in relation to your desk. In era in which most of us work on computers and share information electronically, the relevance of this set-up is an open question.

We sit because **we want to "take a load off."** We feel like the intellectual work that we're doing at our desks is trying enough, that we shouldn't have to tax our body while we're doing office work and that we need to conserve our energy to be productive for the task at hand. (Spoiler alert: Later you will see evidence of the opposite; we actually feel more vital and engaged and are more productive when we do office work while standing or moving.)

We sit because **it's "comfortable."** High-tech, overly designed chairs and other ergonomic innovations cradle us in cozy work cocoons that make us forget that we're sitting all day.

We sit because **employers make us**. You need special gear to stand up and get moving at work and many employers are reluctant to provide it. Even now, nearly a decade after widespread dissemination of information about how deadly sitting is, many employers still require a doctor's note or other documentation before they'll provide you with nonconventional office equipment — if they'll provide it at all.

We sit because **we don't want to call attention to ourselves**. Even in workplaces where standing and other alternative workstations are available, you may be understandably reluctant to be the pioneering standing-desk or treadmill-desk user in your office.

Outside of the office, we sit in the car. We sit to eat. We sit in front of the TV and game console. We sit in front of our home computer to pay bills. Sometimes it seems like every technological and cultural advance of the past century has been designed to take our feet out from under us and drop us into a chair. As noted in the Introduction, when you add up all the time we spend sitting, for most of us it's the majority of our waking day.

From an anthropological perspective, we sit because as we evolved to be active, upright walkers we found that a restful position between lying and standing would let us conserve energy while still keeping an eye on our surroundings.

There are are lots of good explanations for why we sit, plenty of plausible reasons to keep sitting, and certainly a lot of inertia holding you in your chair. So why make the effort to sit less at work?

Oh, that's right, because, as headline after headline has reminded us, "Sitting Is as Deadly as Smoking."

The Science behind "Sitting Disease"

When you look at the science behind these news stories, you find three major bodies of research related to "sitting disease" and sedentariness.

It's worth pausing for a moment to think about the consequences of the diseases for which sitting puts you at risk. I don't want to get too graphic, but it's worth reflecting on the fact that cancer, diabetes, and heart disease are horrific diseases that not only lop years off of your life but also dramatically reduce the quality of your life.

The research shows that taking care of yourself now can mean the difference between living a long, productive, care-free life and a shorter life filled with more doctor visits, hospital stays, and diminished physical capacity. These risks, of course, apply just as much to other health choices that you make. But the evidence shows that, if you have a desk job, improving your office fitness is

3

arguably the most important improvement you can make to enhance your long-term health prospects.

Enough with the fear mongering. On to the research.

- **Epidemiological, population-level studies** look at large numbers of sitters and non-sitters and report on their overall health.
- **Inactivity physiology studies** look at the troublesome physiological mechanisms associated with sitting, the underlying causes of the "sitting disease" identified in the population studies.
- **Intervention research** looks at the effectiveness of specific interventions that limit sedentary time.

Population-Level Research

In 1953 **Jeremy Morris** and his colleagues in London compared the health of trolley drivers and conductors. Both worked the same hours in the same double-decker trolleys, but the drivers sat all day while the conductors were standing and moving most of the time. The more sedentary drivers were twice as likely to get heart disease as the standing, walking, stair-climbing conductors. Morris also observed similar differences between more active "postmen" and less active "telephonists, executive officers, and clerks." His conclusion: "Men in physically active jobs have a lower incidence of coronary heart-disease in middle age than have men in physically inactive jobs. Moreover, what disease the conductors and postmen had was less severe." This study arguably launched the modern field of sedentary studies.

There had been a few random looks into the field before Morris's work. As early as the late 17th Century, the Italian occupational-medicine pioneer Bernardino Ramazzini had noted that messengers who ran from place to place all day had fewer diseases than sedentary cobblers and tailors. In the late 18th Century, researchers in London replicated Ramazzini's findings and also compared the health of other sedentary and non-sedentary workers and found similar results. And in the early 20th Century American doctors began to note an association between physical work and improved health. But it was the publication of Morris's findings in 1953 that really started the rigorous, scientific, ongoing study of sedentary behavior. Morris continued his studies for nearly 50 more years, working well into his eighties and living to the age of 99. Given his long life and knowing his research interests, we can reasonably assume that even as he pursued a scholarly life he somehow managed to remain routinely active at work. The epidemiological case against sitting has grown considerably since Morris's time.

The next big wave of sedentary-studies activity began with research on **TV-watching couch potatoes**. In 1985, William Dietz asked in the journal Pediatrics, "Do we fatten our children at the television set?" He found that television viewing was a likely cause of obesity in children and adolescents. In 1996, Stephen Sidney and his colleagues reported in the Annals of Epidemiology journal that "heavy TV viewing is a modifiable behavior that is associated with increased prevalence of several cardiovascular risk factors." In 2000, Jo Salmon and her colleagues at Deakin University in Australia said that "public health strategies to reduce overweight and prevent weight gain may need to focus on reducing sedentary behaviors such as television viewing in addition to increasing physical activity" A 2001 study by Frank Hu and his colleagues suggested in the New England Journal of Medicine "the importance of reducing sedentary behavior in the prevention of type 2 diabetes." Adrian Cameron and a large team of researchers reported in 2003 on the 1999-2000 Australian Diabetes, Obesity and Lifestyle Study. They found strong associations between obesity and both television viewing time and lower physical activity time that "confirm the influence of sedentary lifestyles on obesity." A similar large study by David Dunstan and another large team in Australia reported in 2010 that "television viewing time is associated with an increased risk of all-cause and CVD [cardiovascular disease] mortality." A 2008 study by Genevieve Healy showed that even very active people who met recommendations for regular exercise had increased metabolic risk factors that rose with TV viewing time. These are just a few of dozens, if not hundreds, of studies that link prolonged sitting in front of a television to obesity, cancer, heart disease, diabetes, and other serious diseases.

Beginning in the 1990's and up until today, researchers have looked beyond television watchers, turning to the more generic problem of **physical inactivity**. Much of this research arose around the observation that sedentary behavior appeared to be an

5

independent risk factor, a problem regardless of your weight, exercise habits, or other fitness measures. In 1999, Steven Blair and Suzanne Brodney found that you can carry a few extra pounds but sill be better off than a thin person who sits all day, or as they put it, "Overweight or obese individuals who are active and fit are less likely to develop obesity-related chronic diseases and have early death than normal weight persons who lead sedentary lives." In 2006, Lyn Steffen and her colleagues noted in their findings from the Minnesota Heart Survey that from 1980-2000 people reported the same amounts of exercise activity but more sedentary time at work. "It is significant that one easily identifiable sedentary activity, namely, sitting at work (instead of standing), increased markedly over 20 years and that, interestingly, men and women who sat less than half the time at work had a lower BMI [body mass index] than those who sat more than half the time." In 2009, Neville Owen and his colleagues reported in their paper "Too much sitting: a novel and important predictor of chronic disease risk?" that "even if people meet the current recommendation of 30 minutes of physical activity on most days each week, there may be significant adverse metabolic and health effects from prolonged sitting." Also in 2009, Peter Katzmarzyk and his colleagues found "a dose-response association [i.e., more of it is worse] between sitting time and mortality from all causes and CVD [cardiovascular disease], independent of leisure time physical activity" and urged physicians to "discourage sitting for extended periods."

I could go on — there are literally hundreds of other studies I could cite (many of them listed in the bibliography at sitless.com) — but you get the idea: Sitting is a huge public health problem. And, unfortunately, it is likely to remain so. As Marc Hamilton said in a 2007 paper in the journal Diabetes, "Given the increasing pace of technological change in domestic, community, and workplace environments, modern humans may still not have reached the historical pinnacle of physical inactivity."

Inactivity-Physiology Research

Marc Hamilton is not just a sedentary-studies prognosticator. He is also the leading pioneer in "inactivity physiology," a new field that looks at the physiological mechanisms that underlie "sitting disease." Epidemiologists have shown that sitting is a problem. Hamilton and his crowd show how it is a problem.

Hamilton coined the phrase "inactivity physiology." A few key concepts have already emerged in this nascent field:

- "Humans naturally require a large amount of time in physical activity throughout the whole day for good health." Forty-five minutes of exercise can't offset ten hours of sitting. You need to move throughout the day.
- We don't spend enough time each day doing any physical activity. Muscular inactivity underlies the unique physiological problems of sitting.
- "The signals harming the body during physical inactivity are specific and distinct from exercise." Too much sitting is not the same as too little exercise.

Even before Hamilton coined the phrase in 2004, researchers were already looking at "inactivity physiology" (even if they weren't calling it that then). Much of the early research in this area came out of the air and space fields, where there is plenty of sitting and inactivity. In the early 1980s, for example, aviation-industry researchers curious about the impact of long-term airline flights found blood-pooling in the calves of people who sat for prolonged periods. Beginning in the 1990s, Joan Vernikos and her colleagues at NASA conducted experiments in which they tried to mimic the weightlessness of space with bed rest, culminating in a paper in 2010 that showed how space travel accelerates the aging process. Vernikos worries now that our sedentary ways may be accelerating the aging of sedentary office workers. Exercise physiologists and others have, of course, also looked at the problems of inactivity.

The upshot of all of this research is a long list of physiological problems associated with sitting. Let's look at some of them.

As soon as you sit down, **electrical activity in your muscles drops almost immediately**. "The muscles go as silent as those of a dead horse," said Hamilton in a 2011 article in the New York Times. Along with the drop in electrical activity comes a decrease in the release from your muscles of enzymes that help regulate blood cholesterol levels. "Good" cholesterol (HDL) levels decrease and "bad" cholesterol (LDL) levels increase, putting you at increased risk for atherosclerosis. The deep muscles that help us stand up and maintain a vertical posture also release enzymes that help regulate your cholesterol levels. As soon as you sit down, you turn off this mechanism. Hamilton is probably the best-known researcher in this area, and he and his colleagues have conducted much of the research on the role of postural muscles in regulating cholesterol levels, which they have shown is related to the regulation of lipoprotein lipase (LPL).

When sitting, you **burn calories at a much lower rate** then when you are standing or walking, putting you at risk for obesity. Another sedentary studies pioneer, James Levine at the Mayo Clinic, estimates that you burn somewhere between 700 and 1000 calories in the typical office job if you sit most of the day and about 1400 calories if you stand most of the day (compared with 2,300 calories in strenuous occupations like farming). Following this math, simply standing instead of sitting most of the day burns enough calories to help you lose about 10 pounds a year, and walking at a leisurely two miles per hour on a treadmill desk could help you lose 40. Looking at this another way, going back to the start of someone's office career, you can see the almost-immediate impact of burning fewer calories. One study, for example, looked at the effects of sedentary work on previously active employees and found that the typical new office employee puts on 16 pounds within 8 months of starting a sedentary desk job.

Reduced moving time and increased sitting time reduces your body's ability to process glucose and **increases your risk for diabetes**. One study found that having non-exercising men reduce their daily number of steps taken from 10,000 to 1,500 for just two weeks significantly reduced their insulin action (Rikke Krogh-Madsen 2010). Another found that "a single day of prolonged sitting can dramatically reduce insulin action in healthy young adults" (Stephens 2011). John Buckley and his colleagues in the UK (2013) conducted the first study to look specifically at the effects of standing vs. sitting in an actual office setting. They found a 43% improvement in blood glucose levels when subjects did their work standing up. (They also found that standing workers burned about 50 more calories per hour).

Sitting has also been implicated in **systemic inflammation**, a prime suspect in many chronic diseases. A 2012 study found chronic low-grade inflammation in women in sedentary occupations (but, curiously, not in men). Given the growing interest in inflammation as a contributing factor in many serious diseases, I predict we'll soon see more research on the role sitting and sedentary behavior on chronic inflammation.

When you sit down, your "second heart" — deep muscles in your calves that help pump blood back up to your heart — is turned off, **impairing your blood circulation**. Those muscles have to be used to do their job, and they are shut down when you sit. Among the many problems this can cause is a very serious, potentially life-threatening condition called deep vein thrombosis. Sitting also also impairs microvascular function. Subtle, regular movements of your body help the tiny blood vessels in your arms and legs work properly. When you sit down and stop moving this microvascular activity drops dramatically, further impairing your circulation.

Sitting also **alters your body's ability to regulate blood pressure**. Joan Vernikos, the former head of Life Sciences at NASA, and her colleagues found that the motion of simply standing up activates mechanoreceptors in your neck that help regulate blood pressure. Plop down in your office chair and stay there for several hours and this mechanism never gets a chance to work.

Sitting physically shortens, lengthens, and otherwise **distorts your muscles, tendons, and ligaments**, and the fascia and other tissues around them, causing postural distortions that lead to everything from low-back pain to headaches. The muscles that flex your hips shorten up as you passively flex them in your chair, causing back trouble when stand up. Your back muscles turn off, causing passive structures like ligaments and intervertebral disks to take up the slack in an attempt to hold you upright, leading to back pain and other conditions. Your intervertebral disk, the big thick pads between each pair of bones in your spine, need regular movement to nourish them, and sitting, of course, prevents this. Adding insult to injury, your hamstrings and buttocks are crushed between your torso above and a poorly designed office chair below. I'll talk much more about these kinds of orthopedic issues later in this chapter as well as in the Posture chapter.

Finally, when you sit down the **muscles that hold you upright flicker off** and forget how to work properly, leaving you at risk for injury when you do try to use them. Perhaps the most dramatic example of this is a "weekend warrior" injury to an underused muscle that snaps under sudden exertion. Personal trainers who work with desk jockeys spend a lot of their time teaching chronic

9

sitters to reengage muscles like these that have atrophied after years of misuse and neglect.

Other physiological problems are associated with sitting, and certainly more will be discovered, but I think you get the idea: Sitting all day is not kind to your body.

Intervention Research

A growing body of emerging research looks at the effects of specific interventions designed to counteract the effects of sitting. Most of the research has been conducted in the past couple of years, so much remains to be learned and discovered in this brand new field. So far, though, it looks like the hypothesis is sound: Moving more and sitting less can improve your health.

Several studies have shown that **breaking up sitting** with light or moderate physical activity every 20 to 60 minutes reduces levels of biomarkers associated with diabetes. Teatske Altenburg, a sedentary studies researcher in The Netherlands, and her colleagues found that interrupting prolonged bouts of sitting with eight minutes of moderately intense bicycling every hour reduced levels of proteins associated with diabetes. Having both a bicycle and ten minutes free every hour isn't typical for most office workers, of course. In a more realistically designed study, David Dunstan, a sedentary-studies researcher in Australia, found that taking a two-minute break every 20 minutes to do "light- or moderate-intensity walking lowers postprandial [after a meal] glucose and insulin levels in overweight/obese adults." So, if you can somehow find a way to take a two-minute walk every twenty minutes (say, by sharing a treadmill desk with your colleagues), you can reduce your risk of diabetes.

Another study, the first of its kind, used a very similar intervention — two minutes of light activity every 20 minutes — to examine the effects of sitting on gene expression in muscles. Celine Latouche and her colleagues at the Baker IDI Heart and Diabetes Institute in Australia found that "breaking up sedentary time with short activity bouts is associated with changes in the expression of skeletal muscle genes involved in cellular development, growth and proliferation, and lipid and carbohydrate metabolism," all of these beneficial. They also "observed similarities between genes regulated by breaks and by continuous acute exercise bouts of 30–90 minutes."

So, at least in terms of genetic expression, regular routine movement may offer benefits similar to those gained by vigorous exercise. By the way, I think the people in this study should be honored in some way, since the research included taking from each of them multiple biopsies, each biopsy entailing being cut open with a scalpel and then having a big needle passed through the opening to retrieve muscle tissue for analysis. Ouch!

One of the most common interventions proposed to break up our sitting days is the **standing desk**. An inordinate number of studies on standing desks have looked specifically at their effects on productivity. This meshes with anecdotal evidence that I have gathered in an amazing number of conversations that go like this: "Oh my God! If I stand up I'll quit thinking," or "I have to sit to think and get my best work done." Is standing to work really as disruptive as trying to rub your belly and pat your head at the same time? The evidence does not support this fear.

A 2009 study by Britta Husemann and her colleagues in Germany found that "a sit-stand workstation paradigm reduces musculoskeletal complaints without considerably affecting data entry efficiency." A 2011 study by Christina Ohlinger and her colleagues at Miami University found evidence that you can indeed think and stand at the same time, demonstrating that standing workstations can "increase physical activity in the workplace without compromising cognitive capabilities." Also at Miami University, Ronald Cox and his colleagues looked at people's ability to speak while sitting, standing, and walking at one mile per hour on a treadmill and found no difference in their ability to speak clearly and grammatically, concluding that "the significant elevation of metabolic rate in the absence of any deterioration in speech quality or RPE [rating of perceived exertion] support the utility of using active workstations to increase physical activity in the work environment." So it looks like you can safely stand upright, think, and even talk while using a standing desk.

Moving beyond concerns about productivity while standing, more recent research is testing whether people office workers will actually use standing desks and what the metabolic effects would be if they did. The first study to look specifically at this was a team lead by Nicholas Gilson at the University of Queensland in Australia. In 2012 they reported that when standing desks were made available most people in the office used them and replaced most of their sitting time with standing time. The only notable change in the biomarkers they examined was a significant increase in HDL (the "good" cholesterol) levels. A 2013 study at Curtin University in Australia replicated the finding that when standing desks were made available, office workers stood more (Straker 2013). Also in 2013, another Australian team of researchers found that sitting time was reduced from 85% of the workday to 60% with the introduction of sit-stand desks in a government office in Sydney (Grunseit 2013). Standing desks may not be for everyone, but it looks like a lot of people will use them if they're available.

The other commonly proposed sitting intervention is, of course, the **treadmill desk**, a combined standing work station and low-speed treadmill that permit you to walk while you work. Several studies have looked specifically at treadmill desks in office settings. As expected, they provide evidence that walking at work burns more calories. A 2008 study in the British Journal of Sports Medicine, for example, reported that treadmill desk users burned an extra 200 calories per day (Thompson 2008). The big hope, of course, is that walking on a treadmill all day will help you get healthier and maybe even look better. The evidence supports that hope. Researchers at the University of Massachusetts found that walking while working "favorably influenced waist and hip circumferences and lipid and metabolic profiles in overweight and obese office-workers" (John 2011).

As is the case with standing desks, treadmill desks cause concern that productivity might decline. Indeed there is some evidence of this. Researchers at Miami University and at the University of Tennessee found that some fine motor skills (using a mouse, for example) were impaired while working at a treadmill desk (a 6-11% reduction in accuracy) and that math skills were somewhat diminished (John 2009). However, these studies found no negative effects on the participants' ability to think, to focus, and to comprehend written works. Another study that looked at radiologists who evaluated CT scans and found that their analyses of those crucial images were just as good when they evaluated them while walking at a treadmill workstation (Fidler 2008).

Many researchers note that because their studies are conducted over relatively short time spans, some of the productivity declines they observe might be mitigated with more training and experience. Researchers at the Mayo Clinic, for example, gave transcriptionists four hours of training before comparing their seated work with treadmill transcriptions. They conclude that "more than 4 hours of training will be necessary to prevent a significant drop in employee productivity" (Thompson 2011).

A couple of studies have looked at **under-desk stepping and pedaling machines**. The most detailed of these, a 2012 study by Lucas Carr and his colleagues at the Centers for Behavioral and Preventive Medicine in Rhode Island, gave full-time office workers under-desk pedaling machines and tracked their usage over four weeks. They found that, without any prompting other than the presence of the gadget, the experiment's participants used it about a half hour every day and reported that it was comfortable and enjoyable and a good indoor exercise for rainy days. The study measured only time spent using the machines, not any of the biomarkers associated with sitting and exercise, and gathered just a little qualitative feedback from the participants, so much more research is needed on these machines. One concern that I have with these gadgets is that they are used sitting down and that they have so far been used only episodically, making them more like an exercise intervention than a sedentariness-reduction intervention. It will be interesting to see whether and how future research untangles the independent threads of sitting versus exercise with this kind of intervention.

One other intervention on the horizon deserves comment: the "metabolic polypill." Pharmaceutical companies are developing a medication that combines aspirin, statins (for managing cholesterol levels), and blood pressure-lowering agents. This pill is designed for patients at high risk for cardiovascular disease, but it has already been proposed as a remedy for "sitting disease." Not surprisingly, many exercise-physiology researchers disagree with this idea. In a paper entitled "Exercise Is the Real Polypill," Carmen Fiuza-Luces and her colleagues note that "regular exercise, a drug-free intervention, is available at low cost and relatively free of adverse effects" and that compared to exercise "no drug intervention has proven efficient to maintain muscle fitness, a key factor to ensure independent living throughout all stages of life." A medication like the polypill might address some of the symptoms of your sitting condition, but it can't help you stay strong and vigorous into your later years, as exercise can.

As you can see, sitting causes plenty of problems, and this section has described a sample of the nascent understanding of what to do about it. As David Dunstan, the oft-cited Australian researcher points out, "Even in physically active adults, concurrent reductions in the amount of time spent sitting is likely to confer health benefits." The rest of this book aims to help you to develop habits that have you routinely move more during your workday or, at the very least, to sit less.

In other words, it's time to get up off your derriere and get moving at work. Are you standing up yet?

* * *

The research shows that moving more at work will almost certainly prevent disease and add quality to each year of your longer life. But office work presents other problems. In addition to being sedentary, office work is also stationary, repetitive, and stressful. Let's look at some of the implications of those characteristics.

Both Sedentariness and Stationariness Are Problems

The difference between being sedentary and being stationary might seem like an overly pedantic distinction, but the distinction matters in the context of office fitness. The word sedentary comes from the Latin *sedentarius*, which literally means "sitting." The word stationary comes from the Latin *stationarius*, which referred to soldiers standing at a post or station. In this book, I use the term sedentary mostly to talk about sitting and stationary to talk about the about more general problem of not moving.

Like sedentariness, being stationary is unkind to your body. We are designed to move. Putting yourself into any one posture or position for hours on end is unnatural and can unnecessarily challenge your body, leading to orthopedic injuries and contributing to other pathological conditions. This, of course, applies to sitting at a desk all day, but it can also apply to the more physiologically engaged but nevertheless stationary posture of standing.

14

The tissues in our bodies constantly adapt to the stresses placed upon them. Early in life the changes can be dramatic. Take a moment to feel the bony knobs at either side of the base of your skull just behind your ears. In infancy those were just tiny buds of bone (anatomically known as the mastoid processes of the temporal bone). When you began to crawl, and lifted your head the muscles attached to that little knob tugged at the buds and gradually pulled them out into their larger shape. Your body created new bone tissue to fill the bigger space. Changes become less dramatic as we age, but they are happening throughout our lives. Our bodies constantly adapt to the outside forces (gravity, furniture, clothing, etc.) and to our movements — or lack thereof. Think about the positive effect that regular exercise has on the way you look and feel. In a cruel and pathological sense, being stationary has the opposite effect.

Effects on the Body

Think about your body's organs and systems and how your sitting or standing still for most of the day could affect your skin (the biggest organ in your body); your circulatory, nervous, and digestive systems; and your muscles and bones.

Skin. Your skin is pulled tautly over your muscles and bones, as if you were wearing a snug unitard covering your entire body. This crucial organ protects you from pathogens and other environmental hazards, senses heat and cold and pain, and performs a variety of other vital functions, many of which can be disrupted when you sit down for prolonged periods. For example, your skin plays an important role in your body's heat regulation, but it needs access your environment to do this. This is why chairs with mesh fabrics feel more comfortable than squishy, close-knit fabrics that closely conform to your body.

Circulatory system. Prolonged sitting or standing can put you at risk for impaired local blood circulation in addition to the circulation problems mentioned in the research summary earlier in this chapter. For example, a common consequence of working at a computer for long stretches is a "dead" feeling in the arms and hands. That sensation is almost always caused by postural changes in the shoulders and thorax that impede blood flow into the arms. Much less common, though still a legitimate concern for office

15

workers, is deep vein thrombosis, a serious circulatory condition that can be caused by prolonged sitting.

Nervous system. That "dead" sensation in your arms after long bouts of computing is usually not solely a circulatory issue. The blood vessels that go into your arms are bundled with the nerves that serve your arms and hands, and those nerves can also be impinged by computer-use posture. In some cases, impingement of those neurovascular bundles leads to a condition known as thoracic outlet syndrome. Similarly, the nerves that go into your legs, in particular the sciatic nerve, can be impinged in the low back and/or hips, leading to sciatica: tingling and pain in your hips and legs.

Digestive system and other internal organs. Just as desk posture can constrict your blood vessels and nerves, sedentary behavior can compromise your internal organs and movement can help them. Researchers have shown, for example, that taking a walk after a meal improves digestion. Picture also your lungs and other internal organs being compressed when you slouch in your desk chair and your rib cage settles onto them.

Musculature. Depending on how you count, the human body has around 800 or 900 muscles. As the source of our movement, these tissues are arguably the most disheartened structures in a sedentary or stationary body. When we sit, not only are the muscles not moving, they can be contorted into unnatural positions which, over time, can lead to postural distortions and cause pain.

Even when not in use, muscles are poised for action, ready to serve us at a moment's notice. In settings less abnormal than office spaces, our bodies rest in relaxed, neutral positions from which we can immediately spring into muscular action. Sedentary and stationary computer postures throw a monkey wrench into this arrangement, shortening some muscle sets and stretching others. Then neither set of muscles can work properly. A muscle already in a shortened position has little space in which to contract much further. A muscle already in a lengthened position has to "take up the slack" before it can fully engage to do its job. Over time, muscles in either situation become resigned to their fate and permanently adopt their shortened or lengthened position.

After days, hours, weeks, months, and years of peering into your computer monitor, pairs of opposing muscles in your shoulders and neck and at the base of your skull can end up shortened and lengthened, leaving you with chronic headaches as well as neck and shoulder pain. Had you been up walking around, picking berries, and chasing rabbits across meadows, this wouldn't have happened.

Skeletal system. Even your bones are affected by a sedentary and stationary work style. Although we think of bones as permanently fixed structures, bones are more flexible and resilient than commonly thought. In fact, recent research shows that bones consist largely of a gooey substance lying between the nano-scale crystals that make up the hard part of bone tissue. Even before this discovery, though, doctors knew that sedentary behavior was a strong risk factor for conditions like osteoporosis.

You can see that whether you're sitting down, standing still, or otherwise staying in one position for long periods, failure to move regularly is unkind to your body.

Office Work Is Repetitive

The little movement that we can manage in a modern office is just that — little. Big, natural movements like walking, running, and climbing propel us through space, using long chains of muscle and connective tissue. They get our heart pumping with movements we've been doing for millennia. Small, unnatural movements like typing and using a computer mouse keep cursors moving and words and numbers and code flowing, but that's about it. Worst of all, we make the same motions over and over and over again.

Repeating these small movements all day long can have a surprisingly big effect on your body. From full-blown carpal tunnel syndrome to achy wrists at the end of a long workday, repetitive strain injuries (RSIs) are a bane of the modern office. They cause outsized amounts of pain and impede office productivity.

Perhaps the most unhealthy thing about these small movements is their repetitive nature. Just as repeatedly bending a wire coat hanger back and forth will eventually snap it in two, repeatedly sliding tendons across bones and other structures can fray them and make them more susceptible to injury. Rotating your palm face down and then repeatedly extending your fingers to make keystrokes sets up exactly this kind of situation. Reaching out for your mouse, even it it's just a couple of inches, and then bending your wrist over and over to operate it, does too.

Using just one part of the body in isolation is what makes those movements unhealthy. The big, natural movements that we have used throughout our history involve long connected chains of muscles and bones and other tissues that support one another. A repeated tiny motion by one part of your body breaks the chains and removes their support.

This, by the way, points to one of the many ways that maintaining a good level of overall fitness can bolster your office fitness. A good level of overall physical robustness can lend support to your body as it struggles to execute tiny, awkward office tasks. In fact, in their analysis of a large Canadian community health survey, Charles Ratzlaff and his colleagues (2007) found that "being physically active during leisure time is associated with a decreased risk of upper-body occupational RSI." (Remember, though, that your leisure-time exercise can't undo the toxic effects of prolonged sedentariness.)

In addition to the general robustness developed by regular exercise, good ergonomics practices and better posture at work can mitigate the damage caused by repetitive motions. Each of these topics gets its own chapter later in this book.

Although I tend to demonize computers and other modern gadgets, repetitive strain injuries have no doubt been around since the first cobbler started cranking out multiple pairs of shoes and the first assembly worker started attaching the same gadget to each car that came down the line. Now, instead of a few thousand people in a few specific fields getting RSIs, tens of millions of office workers are vulnerable because they repeat the same motions over and over again.

Office Work Is Stressful

The modern office is a uniquely stressful place. Ever-rising performance expectations and a relentless flood of information leave you feeling perpetually behind; 24/7 wireless connectivity that lets your work follow you wherever you go, and ever-evolving technology can sap the stress-management resources of even the toughest desk jockey.

The study of psychological stress is a vast, complex undertaking. Allen Elkin, a stress management expert with over 50 years of experience in the field, once wrote that "trying to define stress scientifically is like trying to nail a hunk of jelly to a tree." Nevertheless, I'll attempt a quick overview.

Stress is a normal human response to events and stimuli in the world around us. Good stress (called "eustress" by Hans Selye, a pioneering stress researcher) can be beneficial — motivating, challenging, and energizing us. Think about athletic competition, the imminent launch of your favorite new project, or mustering the courage to attempt a first kiss.

When the demands placed on your mind and body exceed your coping resources — when you are cornered by a hungry tiger, for example — you experience bad stress, or "distress." In distress, your body automatically and rapidly releases a series of hormones that put you in the well-known "fight or flight" mode. Throughout most of human history, the hormonal avalanche unleashed under acute stress was episodic and short-lived. You escaped the tiger and got on with your life. Nowadays, as you may have noticed, our stressors hang around longer.

Your body's immediate responses when you face stress make sense physiologically. Functions irrelevant when a hungry tiger is bearing down on you — like digestion, immunity, and procreation — are put on hold. Functions absolutely necessary in a crisis — like increased alertness, quicker reaction times, more energy, reduced pain perception, and better blood flow — are engaged at full throttle. The end result is a body on high alert, ready for any physical challenge. Your vision narrows, focusing on the threat. Your palms sweat. Your pulse races. Your stomach tightens. Your jaw clenches. Your muscles become engaged and taut. For the time being, you are stronger, have faster reaction times, are extremely focused, are poised to fight or flee.

That is exactly what you need when a tiger is coming after you, but it is rarely a helpful response in the modern office. The stress response mechanism is a short-term tactic, designed to get you away from that tiger or to slay it with your trusty spear. Nowadays, instead of the occasional tiger attack, we face an endless stream of stressors. Faced with long-term stressors, our bodies react as they always have, with those vestigial responses designed to deal with a short-term problem. We end up in bodies that are constantly bathed in hormones that trigger knee-jerk reactions, tunnel vision, high blood pressure, increased heart rate, suppressed immunity, tight muscles, and poor digestion. Not exactly the ingredients for a productive, positive workday.

An effective self-care strategy for dealing with stress in your work life and personal life can obviously not begin and end with this book. I will point out, however, that exercise and movement practices like those I advocate here are generally included in a comprehensive stress-management plan. Exercise practices that specifically include a mind-body component, like yoga and tai chi, can be particularly useful in helping you manage your stress.

In any case, with exercise appearing near the top of the list in almost every stress-management program, the routine movement and exercises suggested later in this book may help you manage your stress. At the very least you will be taking action, not cowering behind a tree, waiting for the tiger to leave.

What to Do about These Hazards

I've hinted at some solutions while discussing these challenges of office work. If you're sedentary and stationary at work, you need to sit less and move more. If you're doing repetitive motions all day, you need to do them correctly. If your work set-up contorts you into positions that created pain and discomfort, you need to improve your posture.

That's what the rest of this book is about. Chapter 3 shows you how to incorporate routine movement into your workday, to reduce your risk of "sitting disease." Chapter 4 shows you how to take charge of your ergonomic set-up, to mitigate the hazards of doing repetitive micro-movements all day. Chapter 5 shows you how to cultivate "body awareness" and improve your posture, to reduce the strain on your body that leads to pain and injury. Chapter 6 shows you exercises that you can do at work, at home, and at the gym both to counteract the effects of your sedentary, repetitive, stressful job and to support your new, improved posture.

But first, Chapter 2 shows you how to create better office fitness habits. After all, these behaviors that are giving us so much trouble are all habits, bad habits that we have unintentionally adopted over the years. Understanding how habits work and how to develop better ones is the master key to office fitness.

Suggested Reading

Sitting Kills, Moving Heals: How Everyday Movement Will Prevent Pain, Illness, and Early Death -- and Exercise Alone Won't, Joan Vernikos

Get Up!: Why Your Chair Is Killing You and What You Can Do About It, James Levine

Sources

"Hans Selye." Wikipedia, the Free Encyclopedia, March 1, 2013.

Altenburg, Teatske M., Joost Rotteveel, David W. Dunstan, Jo Salmon, and Mai J. M. Chinapaw. "The Effect of Interrupting Prolonged Sitting Time with Short, Hourly, Moderate-Intensity Cycling Bouts on Cardiometabolic Risk Factors in Healthy, Young Adults." Journal of Applied Physiology 115, no. 12 (December 15, 2013): 1751–56.

Ashton, John R. "Professor J N 'Jerry' Morris." Journal of Epidemiology and Community Health 54, no. 12 (December 1, 2000): 881–881.

Blair, Steven N. "Physical Inactivity: The Biggest Public Health Problem of the 21st Century." British Journal of Sports Medicine 43, no. 1 (January 1, 2009): 1–2.

Blair, Steven, and Suzanne Brodney. "Effects of Physical Inactivity and Obesity on Morbidity and Mortality: Current Evidence and Research Issues. [Miscellaneous Article]." Medicine & Science in Sports & Exercise November 1999 31, no. 11 (1999).

Buckley, John P., Duane D. Mellor, Michael Morris, and Franklin Joseph. "Standing-Based Office Work Shows Encouraging Signs of Attenuating Post-Prandial Glycaemic Excursion." Occupational and Environmental Medicine, December 2, 2013, oemed–2013–101823.

Cameron, Adrian J, Timothy A Welborn, Paul Z Zimmet, David W Dunstan, Neville Owen, Jo Salmon, Marita Dalton, Damien Jolley, and Jonathan E Shaw. "Overweight and Obesity in Australia: The 1999-2000 Australian Diabetes, Obesity and Lifestyle Study (AusDiab)." The Medical Journal of Australia 178, no. 9 (May 5, 2003): 427–32.

Carr, Lucas J., Kristen A. Walaska, and Bess H. Marcus. "Feasibility of a Portable Pedal Exercise Machine for Reducing Sedentary Time in the Workplace." British Journal of Sports Medicine 46, no. 6 (May 1, 2012): 430–35.

Cox, Ronald Howard, Jared Guth, Leah Siekemeyer, Brianna Kellems, Susan Baker Brehm, and Christina M Ohlinger. "Metabolic Cost and Speech Quality While Using an Active Workstation." Journal of Physical Activity & Health 8, no. 3 (March 2011): 332–39.

Dietz Jr., William H., and Steven L. Gortmaker. "Do We Fatten Our Children at the Television Set? Obesity and Television Viewing in Children and Adolescents." Pediatrics 75, no. 5 (May 1985): 807.

Dunstan, David W., Bethany Howard, Genevieve N. Healy, and Neville Owen. "Too Much Sitting – A Health Hazard." Diabetes Research and Clinical Practice 97, no. 3 (September 2012): 368–76.

Dunstan, David W., Bronwyn A. Kingwell, Robyn Larsen, Genevieve N. Healy, Ester Cerin, Marc T. Hamilton, Jonathan E. Shaw, et al. "Breaking Up Prolonged Sitting Reduces Postprandial Glucose and Insulin Responses." Diabetes Care 35, no. 5 (May 1, 2012): 976–83.

Dunstan, David W., E. L. M. Barr, G. N. Healy, J. Salmon, J. E. Shaw, B. Balkau, D. J. Magliano, A. J. Cameron, P. Z. Zimmet, and N. Owen. "Television Viewing Time and Mortality The Australian Diabetes, Obesity and Lifestyle Study (AusDiab)." Circulation 121, no. 3 (January 26, 2010): 384–91.

Elkin, Allen. Stress Management for Dummies. 1st ed. For Dummies, 1999.

Fidler, Jeff L., Robert L. MacCarty, Stephen J. Swensen, James E. Huprich, Warren G. Thompson, Tanya L. Hoskin, and James A. Levine. "Feasibility of Using a Walking Workstation During CT Image Interpretation." Journal of the American College of Radiology 5, no. 11 (November 2008): 1130–36.

Fiuza-Luces, Carmen, Nuria Garatachea, Nathan A. Berger, and Alejandro Lucia. "Exercise Is the Real Polypill." Physiology 28, no. 5 (September 1, 2013): 330–58.

Gilson, Nicholas D., Alessandro Suppini, Gemma C. Ryde, Helen E. Brown, and Wendy J. Brown. "Does the Use of Standing 'hot' Desks Change Sedentary Work Time in an Open Plan Office?" Preventive Medicine, Special Section: Complementary and Alternative Medicine II, 54, no. 1 (January 1, 2012): 65–67.

Grunseit, Anne Carolyn, Josephine Yuk-Yin Chau, Hidde Pieter van der Ploeg, and Adrian Bauman. "'Thinking on Your Feet': A Qualitative Evaluation of Sit-Stand Desks in an Australian Workplace." BMC Public Health 13, no. 1 (2013): 365.

Hamilton, M. T., D. G. Hamilton, and T. W. Zderic. "Role of Low Energy Expenditure and Sitting in Obesity, Metabolic Syndrome, Type 2

Diabetes, and Cardiovascular Disease." Diabetes 56, no. 11 (September 7, 2007): 2655–67.

Hamilton, Marc T., Genevieve N. Healy, David W. Dunstan, Theodore W. Zderic, and Neville Owen. "Too Little Exercise and Too Much Sitting: Inactivity Physiology and the Need for New Recommendations on Sedentary Behavior." Current Cardiovascular Risk Reports 2, no. 4 (October 17, 2008): 292–98.

Healy, Genevieve N, David W Dunstan, Jo Salmon, Jonathan E Shaw, Paul Z Zimmet, and Neville Owen. "Television Time and Continuous Metabolic Risk in Physically Active Adults." Medicine and Science in Sports and Exercise 40, no. 4 (April 2008): 639–45.

Hu, Frank, Leitzmann MF, Stampfer MJ, Colditz GA, Willett WC, and Rimm EB. "Physical Activity and Television Watching in Relation to Risk for Type 2 Diabetes Mellitus in Men." Archives of Internal Medicine 161, no. 12 (June 25, 2001): 1542–48.

Husemann, Britta, Carolin Yvonne Von Mach, Daniel Borsotto, Kirsten Isabel Zepf, and Jutta Scharnbacher. "Comparisons of Musculoskeletal Complaints and Data Entry between a Sitting and a Sit-Stand Workstation Paradigm." Human Factors 51, no. 3 (June 2009): 310–20.

John, Dinesh, David Bassett, Dixie Thompson, Jeffrey Fairbrother, and Debora Baldwin. "Effect of Using a Treadmill Workstation on Performance of Simulated Office Work Tasks." Journal of Physical Activity & Health 6, no. 5 (September 2009): 617–24.

John, Dinesh, Dixie L. Thompson, Hollie Raynor, Kenneth Bielak, Bob Rider, and David R. Bassett. "Treadmill Workstations: A Worksite Physical Activity Intervention in Overweight and Obese Office Workers." Journal of Physical Activity & Health 8, no. 8 (November 2011): 1034–43.

Katzmarzyk, Peter T, Timothy S Church, Cora L Craig, and Claude Bouchard. "Sitting Time and Mortality from All Causes, Cardiovascular Disease, and Cancer." Medicine and Science in Sports and Exercise 41, no. 5 (May 2009): 998–1005.

Katzmarzyk, Peter T, Timothy S Church, Cora L Craig, and Claude Bouchard. "Sitting Time and Mortality from All Causes, Cardiovascular Disease, and Cancer." Medicine and Science in Sports and Exercise 41, no. 5 (May 2009): 998–1005.

Knight, Joseph A. "Physical Inactivity: Associated Diseases and Disorders." Annals of Clinical & Laboratory Science 42, no. 3 (June 20, 2012): 320–37.

Krogh-Madsen, Rikke, John P. Thyfault, Christa Broholm, Ole Hartvig Mortensen, Rasmus H. Olsen, Remi Mounier, Peter Plomgaard, Gerrit van Hall, Frank W. Booth, and Bente K. Pedersen. "A 2-Wk Reduction of Ambulatory Activity Attenuates Peripheral Insulin Sensitivity." Journal of Applied Physiology 108, no. 5 (May 1, 2010): 1034–40.

Latouche, Celine, Jeremy B. M. Jowett, Andrew L. Carey, David A. Bertovic, Neville Owen, David W. Dunstan, and Bronwyn A. Kingwell. "Effects of Breaking up Prolonged Sitting on Skeletal Muscle Gene Expression." Journal of Applied Physiology 114, no. 4 (February 15, 2013): 453–60.

Levine, James A., Lorraine M. Lanningham-Foster, Shelly K. McCrady, Alisa C. Krizan, Leslie R. Olson, Paul H. Kane, Michael D. Jensen, and Matthew M. Clark. "Interindividual Variation in Posture Allocation: Possible Role in Human Obesity." Science 307, no. 5709 (January 28, 2005): 584–86.

Morris, JN, JA Heady, PAB Raffle, CG Roberts, and JW Parks. "Coronary Heart-Disease and Physical Activity of Work." The Lancet 262, no. 6795 (November 21, 1953): 1053–67.

Ohlinger, Christina M, Thelma S Horn, William P Berg, and Ronald Howard Cox. "The Effect of Active Workstation Use on Measures of Cognition, Attention, and Motor Skill." Journal of Physical Activity & Health 8, no. 1 (January 2011): 119–25.

Owen, N., A. Bauman, and W. Brown. "Too Much Sitting: A Novel and Important Predictor of Chronic Disease Risk?" British Journal of Sports Medicine 43, no. 2 (February 1, 2009): 81–83.

Ratzlaff, C. R., J. H. Gillies, and M. W. Koehoorn. "Work-Related Repetitive Strain Injury and Leisure-Time Physical Activity." Arthritis & Rheumatism 57, no. 3 (April 15, 2007): 495–500.

Salmon, J, A Bauman, D Crawford, A Timperio, and N Owen. "The Association between Television Viewing and Overweight among Australian Adults Participating in Varying Levels of Leisure-Time Physical Activity." International Journal of Obesity & Related Metabolic Disorders 24, no. 5 (May 2000): 600.

Sapolsky, Robert. Why Zebras Don't Get Ulcers, Third Edition. 3rd ed. Holt Paperbacks, 2004.

Shvartz, E, R C Reibold, R T White, and J G Gaume. "Hemodynamic Responses in Orthostasis Following 5 Hours of Sitting." Aviation, Space, and Environmental Medicine 53, no. 3 (March 1982): 226–31.

Sidney, Stephen, Barbara Sternfeld, William L. Haskell, David R. Jacobs Jr., Margaret A. Chesney, and Stephen B. Hulley. "Television Viewing and Cardiovascular Risk Factors in Young Adults: The CARDIA Study." Annals of Epidemiology 6, no. 2 (March 1996): 154–59.

Steffen, Lyn M., Donna K. Arnett, Henry Blackburn, Gaurang Shah, Chris Armstrong, Russell V. Luepker, and David R. Jacobs. "Population Trends in Leisure-Time Physical Activity: Minnesota Heart Survey, 1980-2000." Medicine & Science in Sports & Exercise 38, no. 10 (October 2006): 1716–23.

Stephens, Brooke R., Kirsten Granados, Theodore W. Zderic, Marc T. Hamilton, and Barry Braun. "Effects of 1 Day of Inactivity on Insulin Action in Healthy Men and Women: Interaction with Energy Intake." Metabolism 60, no. 7 (July 2011): 941–49.

Straker, Leon, Rebecca A. Abbott, Marina Heiden, Svend Erik Mathiassen, and Allan Toomingas. "Sit–stand Desks in Call Centres: Associations of Use and Ergonomics Awareness with Sedentary Behavior." Applied Ergonomics 44, no. 4 (July 2013): 517–22.

Thompson, W G, R C Foster, D S Eide, and J A Levine. "Feasibility of a Walking Workstation to Increase Daily Walking." British Journal of Sports Medicine 42, no. 3 (March 2008): 225–228; discussion 228.

Thompson, Warren G., and James A. Levine. "Productivity of Transcriptionists Using a Treadmill Desk." Work: A Journal of Prevention, Assessment and Rehabilitation 40, no. 4 (2011): 473–77.

Vernikos, Joan, and Victor S. Schneider. "Space, Gravity and the Physiology of Aging: Parallel or Convergent Disciplines? A Mini-Review." Gerontology 56, no. 2 (2010): 157–66.

Vernikos, Joan. "Stand Up for Healthy Aging!" Third Age Health, 2011.

Vlahos, James. "Is Sitting a Lethal Activity?" The New York Times, April 14, 2011, sec. Magazine.

Yates, Thomas, Kamlesh Khunti, Emma G. Wilmot, Emer Brady, David Webb, Bala Srinivasan, Joe Henson, Duncan Talbot, and Melanie J. Davies. "Self-Reported Sitting Time and Markers of Inflammation, Insulin Resistance, and Adiposity." American Journal of Preventive Medicine 42, no. 1 (January 2012): 1–7.

This is a partial list of sources consulted as I wrote this chapter, including only items mentioned or referred to above. For a full list of everything I read as I prepared this chapter, please visit sitless.com/chapter1

Chapter 2
Habits and Behavior Change

Think about how you've spent the past hour. Regardless of the time of day you're reading this, I can guarantee that if you could see a video of your recent behaviors, you would be surprised by how much happened almost automatically, driven by habits that you are barely aware of.

If you have a desk job, you have certainly developed some office fitness habits over the years. You've had your head down, doing your job, paying little attention to your ergonomic set-up or any other aspect of your day-to-day routine that might distract you from getting your job done. After all, that's the main reason you are at work — to earn a paycheck, and to keep earning it by accomplishing everything that your job entails.

Your current office fitness habits probably include way too much sitting, with its attendant slouching and slumping. You're likely to be reaching out for your mouse and keyboard, to be peering into your computer monitor at an odd angle, and to be otherwise considering productivity over your health.

As you saw in Chapter 1, the sitting habit is a huge health problem. To live long, productive lives, we clearly must change our office behavior. To break that deadly sitting habit, it is essential at the very least to routinely get up and get moving. Developing habits that make us more aware of our posture and our ergonomic set-ups can address the more immediate pain and discomfort of desk work by encouraging us to add fitness exercises to our workday.

With the right motivation, preparation, and recurring prompts, adding new behaviors to a regular routine can happen rather quickly. Just think how rapidly we developed a recycling habit and started sneezing into our sleeves rather than our hands. It took even less time to become tethered to internet-connected smart phones.

Think about how rare it is now to see people smoking indoors, driving without a seat belt, or leaving their dog's poop on the sidewalk. Those new habits didn't come easy, and we tend to forget that it took practice to make those changes.

Depending on how you define the term and which expert you consult, between 40% and 95% of your behavior is habitual. Habits drive the brand of soap or toothpaste you buy, your eating rituals, the way you navigate a computer desktop, and to how you comport yourself in a weekly check-in meeting. Sometimes it seems that you're completely at the mercy of your habits — and to some extent you are.

Habits once formed are, by definition, almost completely automatic. You have repeated them so often, and have been rewarded so consistently for doing so, that it takes only a tiny nudge to kick them into gear. Every day, you perform hundreds of habitual routines, unconsciously repeat manners that you learned as a child, and drive your car using elaborate procedures that you couldn't describe even as you do them.

Like other habits you have learned, developing better office fitness habits won't be easy. Anyone who has tried to quit biting their nails or to start eating more vegetables knows that. Behavior change isn't as simple as analyzing a problem and quickly implementing a new routine to solve it. But there is encouraging news.

Habitual behavior is better understood now than at any time in history. Researchers and clinicians have uncovered a gold mine of information about how habits work, about how to hack them and how to turn powerful behavior controllers to your advantage. This chapter draws on that treasure trove of scientific knowledge to show you how to develop better office fitness habits.

The Fogg Behavioral Model

Habits are, of course, behaviors. So let's take a quick look at the broader topic of behavior change before we delve into the specifics of habit formation.

B.J. Fogg, a psychologist at Stanford University, has created a tidy model that shows how behavior change works: Three basic elements — motivation, ability, and a trigger — must converge in the same moment to put a new behavior into action.

What Fogg calls triggers are cues or other reminders to perform the desired behavior. A trigger can be anything from an external reminder like a calendar alert to an unconscious cue like walking into your office. Whatever the trigger, when you are exposed to it, you must then be both motivated to engage and capable of performing the desired behavior. Here's how Fogg maps out this terrain for behavior change:

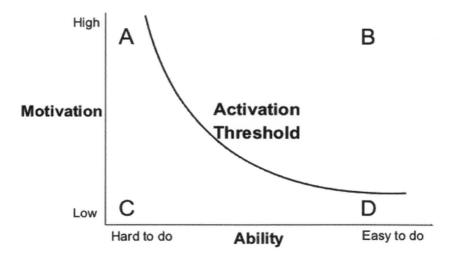

The vertical axis indicates how **motivated** you are to adopt a new behavior. Say, for example, you read dozens of articles about how deadly it is to be chronically dehydrated; your motivation to drink more water will probably be quite high. On the other hand, if you love your three daily deep-fried cheeseburgers and would never give them up regardless of the nutritional evidence, your motivation to change your diet would be low.

The horizontal axis shows the measure of your **ability** to adopt the new behavior. If the desired behavior is completely new to you, difficult to learn, and complicated to execute, your ability will fall toward the left edge of the graph. A familiar behavior that is easy to perform will put your ability toward the right edge of the graph.

Plotting motivation against ability generates the curved line on the graph. This line shows the **activation threshold** at which a trigger is likely to work. Say, for example, you sort of maybe might want to replace your deeply entrenched daily cheeseburger habit with three healthy homemade meals but you have no idea where the supermarket's produce is, much less how to slice a cucumber. The Fogg model would show your motivation near the bottom of the vertical axis and your ability on the left end of the horizontal axis. Changing your eating behavior will fall below the activation threshold and change simply won't happen regardless of how obvious the trigger is (Point **C** on the graph).

On the other hand, if you are convinced that chronic dehydration is slowly killing you, your motivation is near the top on that axis. Because you know that all you have to do is take a few sips from your water bottle every hour, your ability will show up on the right side of the ability axis. Then the new behavior is very likely to be triggered by even the most subtle reminder (Point **B** on the graph).

Motivation and ability must both be present. Say you are in your car, glance at the dashboard, and realize that you are almost out of gas. You have an important destination to reach, so you are highly motivated to fill the tank, but you are on a busy freeway and the next exit is 25 miles away. Despite your high motivation, your ability to fill the tank in that moment is zero; and that prevents the gas gauge trigger from working (Point **A** on the graph).

One last example: You're in the market for a new computer, browsing the web, and come across a banner ad for a nice-looking laptop. To learn more, all you have to do is click on the ad, but your motivation is diminished by prior experience with pop-up ads and misleading online marketing practices. Despite the simplicity of the task, your motivation is insufficient to activate your ability to click on the ad (Point **D** on the graph).

As you begin to cultivate improved office fitness habits, keep this model in mind. You can even get a sense of how easy or difficult you'll find it to adopt a new habit by drawing your own graph for each desired behavior. Simply sketch out Fogg's chart, gauging your motivation and ability to perform the desired behavior and think through which triggers can set it off. If you find yourself lacking the inclination or ability to execute the new behavior, figure out what you can do to boost your motivation and/or increase your proficiency so that you can cross the trigger-activation threshold. You must cross that threshold for a new behavior to have any chance of becoming a habit.

Habits Defined

Crossing the activation threshold ensures that you can execute the new behavior. When you encounter the trigger and execute the behavior on autopilot, that's when you have a new habit.

One of the key characteristics of a habit is its automatic nature: You effortlessly and unthinkingly just do it when triggered. Some sort of cue or reminder always sets off its automaticity. You finish breakfast and automatically brush your teeth. You sit down in the car and automatically buckle your seat belt. You turn on your computer and automatically check your email. All are behaviors that you once had to think about doing; now they happen almost involuntarily.

To briefly flesh out the definition habit: The word can describe anything from a hand-washing ritual to a career rut, from a customary coffee-shop order to a drug addiction, from housecleaning routines to the customs of a community. This chapter's working definition of a habit: *A behavioral routine cued by an identifiable trigger that has been repeated often enough to become almost completely automatic.*

How to Develop Office Fitness Habits

Each of the substantive chapters later in this book ends with a list of ideas for habit-formation projects. These suggestions range from Tiny Habits that you can easily and immediately incorporate into your life to huge plunges that can truly rock your world.

- **Tiny Habits** are simple new behaviors you can quickly add to your life.
- **Routines** are existing behavior patterns that you can modify to establish new habits.
- **Practices** are established disciplines that can help you create and support desired new behaviors.
- **Plunges** are radical departures that toss you into new circumstances.

I offer that range of ideas because each habit-formation project is unique, because I simply don't know what's going to work for you, and because your needs will change over time. In my massage and training practice (and many other contexts) I rarely, if ever, have exactly the one right solution for my client. That's why I always explore multiple options. When I refer someone to another health-care provider, I always provide at least two names. When I suggest an exercise regimen, I always show several ways to get the desired result. When I'm working with a massage client on an injury or pain pattern, I use a variety of bodywork styles to see which works best.

When it comes to making a long-term, fundamental change, no one knows better than you the particular practice, tactic, or strategy that will work best for you. You yourself may need to try several options to find what works best. That is why each chapter ends with laundry lists of ideas. You can apply one or more of the frameworks I set out in this chapter to come up with your own lists of ideas. Be creative. Many other practices and habits are sure to occur to you as your read.

Add a Tiny Habit

The quickest and simplest framework for behavior change is the "Tiny Habits" method set out by B.J. Fogg, the Stanford psychologist whose model is described at the start of this chapter.

A Tiny Habit is a new behavior that is paired with an existing behavior, that you do at least once a day, that takes less than 30 seconds to accomplish, that requires little effort — and that always comes right after established behavior.

Applying these criteria, Fogg created this model:

"After I [existing habit/anchor], I will [new tiny behavior]."

For example: "After I brush my teeth, I will floss one tooth." Yes, your desired new Tiny Habit should actually be that small.

The keys to ensuring the success of a Tiny Habit are to:

- Pick a **reliable anchor habit**, something you actually already do automatically and routinely.
- Tie the new behavior to a very **specific existing behavior**. Not "after dinner," for example, which is too vague, but rather, "after I load the dishwasher," which is much more specific.
- Similarly, be **specific about the new behavior** you are trying to turn into a habit. "Lose weight" is far too vague and isn't a

single behavior. "Select a smaller dinner plate" is much more specific.

- Your specific behavior should be **truly easy** to do. Fogg writes, "The easier the behavior, the less it depends on motivation."
- Match the new behavior with an anchor behavior that **happens about as often** as you'd like to do the new behavior. Flossing after you brush is a good example. To be effective, anchor more frequently desired behaviors to existing habits that you do throughout the day, for example, "after I go to the bathroom" or "after I hang up the phone."
- Make sure to link the desired behavior and the anchor behavior **thematically and logically**. Brushing and flossing naturally go together. But loading the dishwasher and answering emails are not at all alike, so you probably wouldn't pair them up.
- **Celebrate** your accomplishment each time you do the new behavior. Regular, positive reinforcement is crucial to the success of any new habit. Fogg says, "The stronger you feel a positive emotion after your Tiny Habit, the faster it will become automatic in your life." He suggests doing a quick gesture, movement, or vocalization — like a fist pump, a little dance, or self-congratulation (aloud or silently) like "Awesome!" or "I rock!"

Note how the elements of Tiny Habits line up with Fogg's Behavior Model. Tiny Habit behaviors are easy, so you're way to the right on the ability axis. By their nature, they require little or no conscious motivation, no pep talks or other jump-starting needed, so you automatically float to the top of the motivation axis. So when they are triggered by your existing habit, they are easy to actually do. You're way up in the upper right part of the Behavior Model graph where behavior change is easy.

Modify a Habit Loop

A more elaborate framework for behavior change is the habit-loop-hacking method.

In his book, *The Power of Habit*, Charles Duhigg dissects habitual behaviors. To show how a habit can be formed, he uses the introduction of Pepsodent toothpaste. A hundred years ago, people didn't routinely brush their teeth, even though toothbrushes and toothpaste had been around for years. Claude Hopkins, the advertising executive behind the Pepsodent launch campaign, did his research as he prepared to promote the new product. He discovered that teeth are normally coated with a film called mucin plaque. You can feel it any time you pass your tongue across your teeth. Hopkins turned this harmless substance into a cue to brush your teeth. "Just run your tongue across your teeth," read one of his ads. "You'll feel a film — that's what makes your teeth look 'off color' and invites decay." The remedy Hopkins offered was to brush your teeth — with Pepsodent, of course.

Duhigg uses this story to illustrate three key elements of a habit:

- an environmental or behavioral **cue** that reminds you to do a behavior, in this example the film you feel on your teeth,
- a **routine** set into action in the presence of the cue, in this example brushing your teeth to remove the film, and
- the **reward** for doing the routine, in this case sparkling, shiny, non-filmy teeth.

The Pepsodent campaign made Hopkins incredibly wealthy, but as insightful and successful as he was, Hopkins had missed one important component of the habit he had created. Underlying the behavior in the loop was a **craving** for the tingly sensation on the gums created by oils and chemicals in the Pepsodent. Other toothpaste manufacturers quickly caught on to the habitual consumer desire for tingling, added similar ingredients, and soon caught up to Pepsodent in the market. In fact, to this day, nearly all toothpastes contain ingredients that have nothing to do with dental hygiene in order to feed that craving for a tingling sensation.

Duhigg sets out a framework in his book to apply knowledge of the habit loop to your own behavior. Note that a framework is a guide to applying some principles, not a recipe like Fogg's Tiny Habits. Fogg's recipe is a way to add new behaviors. Duhigg's framework can help you modify an existing habit loop.

Identify the Routine

The heart of any habit loop is the routine, the actual behavior you do on autopilot. People generally think of it as a "bad habit" to change. Using Duhigg's framework, the first step is to determine exactly which specific behavior you want to change. For example, say you find yourself putting on a few extra pounds. Upon reflection, you realize that you haven't changed your mealtime behavior, but you do have a new habit of heading to the coffee shop every afternoon for a latte. Some quick math reveals that your new beverage habit adds 1,500 calories every week, the equivalent of a couple of full meals. That might very well explain the new padding around your waist. As soon as you have identified the specific behavior that you want to change, some obvious questions arise. Why am I doing this? What is the cue that sends me to Starbucks every afternoon? And what reward am I getting for this behavior? Then you put on your scientist hat and start to run some experiments.

Experiment with Rewards

Rewards satisfy the cravings that underlie a habit loop. Duhigg points out how hard it can be to identify those cravings. Like that now-familiar tingling in the tooth brushing habit loop, cravings often seem obvious in hindsight, but they can be difficult to find in the midst of a behavior-change project. Luckily, you can infer the underlying craving in a habit loop by figuring out which reward you get from that habit.

Simple experiments can identify the rewards. Begin with a dispassionate data-collection period. Don't worry at this point about the specific outcome of your efforts. Just mix up your habit loop by trying different routine-reward combinations. As in any good experiment, those combinations are driven by a hypothesis. So first you need to reflect a bit on what might be going on in the habit loop. When you automatically get up and go to Starbucks, are you hungry? Is your energy flagging? Are you bored? Do you crave human contact?

Next, test your hypotheses. To test the hunger hypothesis, try going to the break room and eat an apple or a candy bar instead of going for a latte. To test the low-energy hypothesis, go back to

Starbucks, but have a cup of black coffee. To test the boredom hypothesis, you might stay at your desk and visit your favorite cute-cat-video website. To test the human contact hypothesis, walk down the hall and visit a colleague.

Then look for patterns. Duhigg recommends setting a timer that goes off fifteen minutes after each time you try a new routine. When the timer goes off, quickly jot down the first three things that occur to you. Once you have collected notes on a few instances of each hypothetical routine, look for patterns in the notes, which should let you figure out the reward you actually crave. For example, if your notes show that you're still bored after watching the cat videos and still feeling low-energy after the cup of black coffee, those probably don't get at the underlying craving. But if you feel rejuvenated and refreshed after walking down the hall to visit with a colleague, that could indicate that simple human contact is what you crave.

Isolate the Cue

Once you have a sense of your routine and how you are being rewarded, isolate the specific cue that triggers that behavior. It can be difficult to find a solitary cue amid all of the stimuli and activity of a typical office worker's day. Fortunately, it turns out that nearly all habit cues fall into one of five categories: location, time, emotional state, other people, and immediately preceding actions. So, as soon as you feel the urge to go get a latte (or other habitual routine), jot down:

- Where you are
- What time it is
- How you feel
- Who else is around
- What you just did

Do this for a week or two and a pattern will almost certainly emerge. You might notice, for example, that it doesn't matter where you are, how you feel, who you're with, or what you just did. The urge always hits between 3:00 and 3:30. You've found your cue, the time of day.

Have a plan

Once you identify each of the three components of the habit loop you want to change, you can make a plan to change the behavior. Recall the sequence of a habit loop: A cue prompts you to do a routine in order to get a reward that satisfies an underlying craving. Drawing on your observations, you can create a plan for modifying your habit. Drawing on the examples above, for example, you might write:

Every day at 3:00 (the time cue you isolated) I will walk down the hall and find a colleague (the routine you identified) to talk with (thereby enjoying the human-contact reward you discovered).

Then put a reminder in your calendar to execute that plan every day at 3:00. As will happen in any habit-change project, you will no doubt slip back into your old habit once or twice. You may ignore your calendar-reminder cue some days. But after a couple of months you are likely to find that, without consciously thinking about it, you automatically get up from your desk at 3:00 every afternoon and go visit a colleague.

Adopt a Practice

Another framework for behavior change is to adopt a practice that supports your desired habit. A practice is a "repeated performance or systematic exercise for the purpose of acquiring skill or proficiency." Think of the many you may have been exposed to, such as exercise, yoga, dance, meditation, and others. The systematic and repetitive nature of practices makes them a great vehicle for adopting new habits.

Most practices have long and established traditions, so you can easily slip into them to develop skills that support your desired new office fitness habits. For example, tapping into a practice like yoga or Pilates can help you more quickly develop better posture habits than if you tackled the project from scratch. Practices can, of course, become habits themselves. But my intention in including them in the lists at the end of each chapter is to provide well-established frameworks in which to cultivate some skills that can help you become more fit at work.

Many practices are associated with founders who attained guru status: Jack LaLanne in the exercise world, Esther Gokhale in the posture world, and Pete Egoscue in the ergonomics world, for example. If you find a guru whose style and approach resonate with you, by all means, jump on their bandwagon (just don't join any cults, please).

Take a Plunge

The most radical framework for behavior change is taking a plunge. Good reasons abound for shaking things up once in a while.

Making a big change like taking a new job, getting married, or moving to a new city immediately changes a huge number of environmental and contextual cues that drive many habits. That makes it easier to change existing habits or to adopt new ones.

In *Switch: How to Change Things When Change Is Hard*, Dan and Chip Heath point out how much easier it is to change when you step into an entirely new context. Even a short-term change like a vacation can help. For example, in *The Power of Habit* Charles Duhigg notes that smokers find it easier to quit when they're on vacation.

I don't want to be too subversive, but it I will point out that the office is likely to remain a tough place to be physically active for the foreseeable future. So, if it suits your ability and temperament and if it works for your family's finances, the best move for your long-term physical fitness might be to change to a career that involves less desk work and more routine movement. For me, doing massage for a living has been a lot kinder to my body than the office work I used to do. (Note that I have been a half-time office worker while writing this book. Practicing what I preach — standing to work, moving regularly, monitoring my posture, etc. — has kept me happier, more productive, and thinner than I would have been in a conventional office work style.)

It is possible, even in the office, to shake things up and create more opportunities to be fit at work — getting a standing desk or a treadmill desk, for example, or helping to create a cultural shift that makes standing and walking meetings the norm. That is, after all, the whole point of this book. So look for many more ideas at the end of each of the following chapters.

A dramatic plunge can invigorate you like a dive into a cool mountain lake.

* * *

At the end of the chapters on routine movement, ergonomics, posture, and exercise you will find a few examples of each of habit-forming methods. These are just my ideas, and you are no doubt smarter and more creative than I. At the very least, you know your life and work style infinitely better than I ever could, so I am confident that you will come up with better tiny habits, more clever routine hacks, wiser practices, and crazier plunges than I can imagine.

Bear in mind that ultimately you want new behaviors to become true habits, to disappear into the background, and to become part of that 40-95% of your life that happens automatically and habitually. Please, as you move forward with new office fitness behaviors, regularly take some time to reflect on and appreciate your new habits.

Suggested Reading

The Power of Habit: Why We Do What We Do in Life and Business, Charles Duhigg

Switch: How to Change Things When Change Is Hard, Chip Heath and Dan Heath.

Change or Die: The Three Keys to Change at Work and in Life, Alan Deutschman

Influencer: The Power to Change Anything, Kerry Patterson, Joseph Grenny, David Maxfield, Ron McMillan, and Al Switzler

The Antidote: Happiness for People Who Can't Stand Positive Thinking, Oliver Burkeman

Willpower: Rediscovering the Greatest Human Strength, Roy Baumeister and John Tierney

Drive: The Surprising Truth About What Motivates Us, Daniel Pink

Sources

"Neurogenesis." Wikipedia, the Free Encyclopedia, July 9, 2013.

"Neuroplasticity." Wikipedia, the Free Encyclopedia, July 9, 2013.

"Self-Efficacy." Wikipedia, the Free Encyclopedia, July 12, 2013.

Baumeister, Roy F., and John Tierney. Willpower: Rediscovering the Greatest Human Strength. New York: Penguin Books, 2012.

Burkeman, Oliver. The Antidote: Happiness for People Who Can't Stand Positive Thinking. New York: Faber and Faber, 2012.

Deutschman, Alan. Change or Die: The Three Keys to Change at Work and in Life. New York: Collins, 2008.

Duhigg, Charles. "Keystone Habits," Chapter 4 in The Power of Habit: Why We Do What We Do in Life and Business. 1st ed. Random House, 2012.

Duhigg, Charles. "The Power of a Crisis," Chapter 6 in The Power of Habit: Why We Do What We Do in Life and Business. 1st ed. Random House, 2012.

Fogg, BJ. "BJ Fogg's Behavior Model." BehaviorModel.org. Accessed January 12, 2014.

Fogg, BJ. "Sandbox (private Blog)." Tiny Habits. Accessed March 4, 2014. http://tinyhabits.com/sandbox/

Heath, Chip, and Dan Heath. Switch: How to Change Things When Change Is Hard. 1st ed. Crown Business, 2010.

Isaac, Brad. "Jerry Seinfeld's Productivity Secret." Lifehacker. Accessed July 6, 2013. http://lifehacker.com/281626/jerry-seinfelds-productivity-secret

Judah, Gaby, Benjamin Gardner, and Robert Aunger. "Forming a Flossing Habit: An Exploratory Study of the Psychological Determinants of Habit Formation." British Journal of Health Psychology 18, no. 2 (2013): 338–53.

Lally, Phillippa, Cornelia H. M. van Jaarsveld, Henry W. W. Potts, and Jane Wardle. "How Are Habits Formed: Modelling Habit Formation in the Real World." European Journal of Social Psychology 40, no. 6 (2010): 998–1009.

Maltz, Maxwell. Psycho-Cybernetics; A New Way to Get More Living Out of Life. 1ST edition. S.l.: Prentice Hall Trade, 1960.

Norman, Donald A. "Categorization of Action Slips." Psychological Review 88, no. 1 (1981): 1.

Paiva, Andrea L., James O. Prochaska, Hui-Qing Yin, Joseph S. Rossi, Colleen A. Redding, Bryan Blissmer, Mark L. Robbins, et al. "Treated

Individuals Who Progress to Action or Maintenance for One Behavior Are More Likely to Make Similar Progress on Another Behavior: Coaction Results of a Pooled Data Analysis of Three Trials." Preventive Medicine 54, no. 5 (May 1, 2012): 331–34.

Phelps, Michael. Michael Phelps: Beneath the Surface. First Edition edition. Champaign, IL: Sports Publishing LLC, 2005.

Wood, Wendy, and David T. Neal. "A New Look at Habits and the Habit-Goal Interface." Psychological Review 114, no. 4 (2007): 843–63.

This is a partial list of sources consulted as I wrote this chapter, including only items mentioned or referred to above. For a full list of everything I read as I prepared this chapter, please visit sitless.com/chapter2

Chapter 3
The Antidote to Sitting Disease

If you work in an office, the most important thing you can do for your long-term health is to get moving at work. The research is persuasive: Less sitting and more moving is the way to prevent "sitting disease."

Routine movement increases circulation, burns calories, builds muscle, improves joint mobility, and encourages bone formation. It aids digestion, moderates blood-sugar and cholesterol levels, and enhances immune system function. All of which help keep "sitting disease" at bay.

The Trouble with Laborsaving Devices

Back in Paleolithic times, we had to hunt or fish for our protein and gather and harvest by hand our almonds and cassava and greens. We often walked for miles to get to a water source or berry bush. But there's no need to go that far back to find more routinely active lifestyles. Until about 50 years ago, daily life routine involved much more physical activity.

The sedentary health hazards of the modern office are the logical, and tragic, culmination of decades of advances in laborsaving technology. Our parents and grandparents lived in homes stocked with hand-cranked devices like meat grinders and washing machines. They walked to the store. They got up and walked across the room to change TV channels — or to adjust the rabbit ears to clear up the reception. Cooks stood over a stove stirring pots to prepare dishes, instead of popping them in a microwave oven. Pet owners bent over to scoop dog food into a dish, instead of using an automatic dispenser. Friends zipped across the room to answer the phone before a caller gave up (or, later, before the answering machine picked up). Kids made up games in sandlots instead of sitting on the couch playing video games. When a baby whimpered in the middle of the night, her mom or dad walked across the hall instead of rolling over to glance at a monitor. Even couch potatoes had to browse the aisles of a video store; now they can simply click on a link at Netflix or Hulu. The list goes on and on — leaf blowers, garage door openers, electric car windows, snow blowers, escalators, and elevators all keep us from moving as much as we used to. Technological advances have successfully removed thousands and thousands of calories worth of activity from our lives.

I'm not suggesting that you go back to pounding laundry on rocks in the river. But when you calculate the amount of energy that our modern laborsaving devices "save" us, it is easy to see why we're putting on weight and getting sicker. We simply need to be more routinely active, at home and at work to recapture our health and vitality.

Arguably the most insidious laborsaving device for office workers is the modern networked computer. Only a few years ago, before computer networks, we still stood up to walk to a filing cabinet to store and retrieve documents. To do research you walked around a library and lifted books and bound collections of journals down from shelves. Old-fashioned typing was a vigorous physical activity compared to the gentle key tapping and screen swiping of today. To send a long report to a colleague in another city, you carried packages of documents to the mailroom; today you hit the "send" key. Layout artists and graphic designers stood at a drawing board to actually cut and paste slips of paper to cardboard to create newspaper and magazine pages and ads. Accountants flipped open heavy binders full of paper spreadsheets. Even computers used to require more human power. In the old days, computer operators had to physically carry trays full of punch cards across the room to input data or alter programs. None of these were exercise activities, but they got us out of our chairs, onto our feet, and moving about throughout the workday.

Moving is NEAT

Sedentary-studies pioneer and Mayo Clinic obesity researcher James Levine highlights the importance of non-exercise activities. Levine coined the acronym NEAT (Non-Exercise Activity Thermogenesis) to describe "the energy expenditure of all physical activities other than volitional sporting-like exercise." NEAT describes any activity that is not completely sedentary but that doesn't cross the threshold into full-on exercise. Although your body is always burning a few calories, even when you're sleeping or sitting down, it burns considerably more as soon as you start to move.

Picture the range of daily human behavior. At one end of the spectrum is such completely inactive behavior as lying in a hammock, at the other is such all-out exertion as competing in a triathlon. Between these extremes are a number of other sedentary behaviors, like sitting in an office chair all day, and a number of lighter exercise behaviors, like jogging or your Zumba class.

The benefits of adding more NEAT activities to your day can add up surprisingly quickly. Levine and his research team discovered that just a few hours of non-exercise activities burn as many calories as 45 to 60 minutes of vigorous activity. "Society keeps building gyms to help us combat obesity," says Levine, "but the calories we burn behind their mirrored walls pale in comparison to those we could and should be burning in normal life."

And NEAT is not only about burning calories and losing weight. "The heart of NEAT," says Levine, "is living your life the way you were meant to live it — out of your chair, on your feet, doing things. It's the difference between sitting down, passively letting life pass you by, and getting up and engaging it full steam."

Traditional farmers walk around 15,000 steps per day. The typical, modern, car-driving office worker takes only around 5,000 steps. Let's see if we can catch up to those farmers.

How to Get Moving at Work

We've known about the hazards of sedentary behaviors for over a decade. Now we're starting to find ways to get moving at work. Some NEAT practices that other office workers have come up with include standing up to work, moving while they work, using

45

devices such as treadmills or exercise bicycles at their desks, or simply standing up and pacing while talking on the phone. Some office teams hold meetings while standing up, walking, even running. The following sections show how to incorporate these and other movements into your workday.

Stand Up to Work

Levine says, "If sitting is the problem, standing is the answer." Standing isn't really moving, of course, but it is better than sitting, and it's definitely NEAT. Standing burns more calories than sitting. It also cranks up your "second heart" — deep muscles in your lower leg that help pump blood back up to your heart. Standing up also engages deep postural muscles that produce enzymes that help regulate your cholesterol levels. Olli Tikkanen (2013) and his colleagues in Finland found that simply "replacing sitting by standing can considerably increase cumulative daily muscle activity."

Being vertical and on your feet also provides more opportunities to move. I have written almost all of this book at a standing desk, but I have rarely stood still for more than a few minutes at a stretch. I walk in place, do simple dance steps, sink into a shallow lunge, squat halfway down into a perching position, and otherwise keep my body engaged and moving as much as possible.

The ideal standing desk is easily height adjustable so that you can both sit and stand and even try intermediate positions like perching. Sit-stand desks come in a variety of styles and in models that can be adjusted manually, electrically, or hydraulically. Their price is dropping every day, so they are now a viable option for even the most budget-conscious people and organizations.

Standing for long periods can get uncomfortable, as generations of assembly-line workers, grocery-store clerks, and highway toll takers have discovered. Fortunately, their experiences with long-term standing have produced practices and gadgets that mitigate the discomfort. Anti-fatigue mats and comfortable shoes can ease foot and knee pain, for example, and a footrest can prevent low-back pain (there is much more on this in the ergonomics chapter).

Also, as the character Dwight Schrute once said on the TV comedy "The Office" in an episode in which he is working at a standing desk, "Standing is proven to be healthier, increases productivity, and just looks cooler."

Work at a Treadmill Desk

Walking is the most natural human activity. If we could just get more of it into our office routines, our caloric expenditures and other metabolic activity could return to near-normal levels. Working on a treadmill desk at a standing-style workstation, you stroll at a slow, non-exercise pace, typically somewhere between one and two miles per hour. The treadmill for a walking workstation has a lower-profile and different gearing than an exercise treadmill, so you won't feel like you're working out at the gym. By walking at such a leisurely pace, you can easily spend most of your workday walking.

The research shows that treadmill desks are safe and that productivity is impaired only a little when working while walking — and the impairment is only for projects that require precise hand motions. Work that requires fine motor control, like graphic design, may be affected (which makes sense if you think about the natural arm swing that comes with walking). But you can type, read, and do most other common work activities at a treadmill desk with little or no ill effect.

Treadmill desks aren't cheap, and they take up a bit more space than a traditional workstation. They also require a bit more maintenance than a conventional desk. One way to defray these costs is to share a treadmill desk with colleagues. Even small amounts of walking at work are beneficial, so breaking up your day with short walking stints on a shared treadmill workstation is one way to get moving if you're on a budget. Just as folks at the gym catch up on TV shows while they jog on the treadmill, you can walk as you read reports or catch up on your email.

Too little data is available at this point to make specific claims about the costs of a treadmill workstation versus its benefits. Nevertheless, here's one data point: medical care for diabetes (a common condition in sedentary workers) typically costs about $10,000 a year. If you could prevent that with a one-time investment of around $2,000 and annual maintenance of around $250, wouldn't that make sense?

Pedal While You Work

As the hazards of sedentary work have become widely known, many do-it-yourselfers and exercise product manufacturers are creating workstations that incorporate bicycles, under-desk pedaling devices and elliptical trainers, and similar exercise devices. Some of those gadgets even use the office worker's pedaling energy to generate electricity.

While pedaling solutions offer the advantage of letting you move at your desk, it's not clear how many workers will find them comfortable or what effect they might have on productivity. Don't get me wrong; I love the idea of these set-ups, but I suspect that they might limit the tasks that you can do while using them. As noted in Chapter 1, to this point there is little scientific research on such products, so no one can yet say just how viable these solutions are. Unlike the natural movement of walking at a treadmill desk or simply standing up, the movements required for these exercise devices are more contrived than working at a standing or treadmill desk. Pedaling devices will probably undergo more scientific scrutiny before they become widely adopted.

You also operate most of the pedal workstation devices while seated, so they don't give you the postural benefits of more natural activities like standing and walking. Despite those drawbacks, they don't appear to present obvious hazards, and many of those gadgets are very affordable — several under-desk pedaling devices cost less than $50. So there's little physical or financial risk in trying them out.

Conduct Standing Meetings

In the world of agile software development, scrum teams have for years used daily standing meetings as a productivity method. That way, they can quickly catch up on each other's activities and identify any obstacles that prevent team members from completing their assignments. Such meetings are very short — 5 to 15 minutes — and tightly focused. You can probably think of a few routine gatherings in your office that could be conducted this way. That doesn't mean that you must adopt the exact format of a scrum check-in meeting, of course. If you want to break up your sitting day and quickly catch up with some of your colleagues, push back the conference room chairs and hold all or part of your next meeting standing up.

Conduct Walking (or Running) Meetings

Even better than the standing meeting is the one the gets you out and about. Walking meetings let you escape both the crummy lighting and the droning HVAC in the conference room — and they give you the opportunity to move naturally. There are, of course, some logistical limitations to the walking meeting. If your meeting requires a slide presentation or other special equipment or facilities, you might not be able to take it on the road. But if you and one or two or three colleagues simply have to discuss something, then get out of the conference room and get moving. Outdoors is best, of course, assuming the weather is reasonable and there is a safe and relatively quiet place to walk as a group. If you need to take notes, one of you can use a portable recorder or a voice memo app on your smart phone. Better yet, if you have colleagues who share your joy of jogging, pick up the pace and go for a quick run as you work out the Q4 budget details.

Stand Up (and Pace) to Take Phone Calls

This is a classic "tiny habit," and it will, of course, make the list at the end of this chapter. Whenever your phone rings, simply stand up to answer it. If you have a cordless headset and a little room to move, you can also pace around your office as you talk. You don't necessarily have to stand up for entire call. Even if the call requires that you sit down to look something up on your computer, you will at least have had the benefit of changing position, unfolding your flexed body, and setting off the blood-pressure-regulation and other physiologically beneficial effects that come with simply standing up.

Stand Up to Read

If you have a standing desk, this is a no-brainer. But whenever you are reading, whether it's a long email, a report, an article, or a book, look for ways to stand while you read. If you work at a laptop, set it down on a standing-height counter or filing cabinet. If you can read your work documents on a tablet or other hand-held gadget, simply stand up at your desk or find a quiet, well-lit corner of the office to read in. Of course you can also stand to read old-fashioned paper documents.

Change Positions Regularly

Standing isn't the be-all and end-all of office fitness. Neither is treadmill desking or the occasional walking meeting. Standing isn't the opposite of sitting; more accurately, moving is the opposite of being sedentary. Similarly, no one movement is the opposite of being stationary; routinely changing positions is the opposite of being stationary. Our bodies are in a valiant ongoing fight against gravity. In her research on the effects of weightlessness, former NASA life sciences chief Joan Vernikos discovered that simply moving from position to position is a significant and important type of non-exercise activity. That is why my dream workstation includes a sit-stand height-adjustable desk that goes low enough that I can squat and high enough that I can stand, and also has a treadmill, a kneeling chair, and other gadgets that let me change positions throughout the workday.

Walk to Colleague's Office instead of Calling

Sometimes we get so enamored of our multi-channel communications technology that we forget that a human being is at the other end of the line, even when that person is right down the hall or up a flight or two of stairs. There's no better way to correct this misconception than to walk to a co-worker's office to ask a quick question or deliver a bit of news.

Also, think about how often a good idea or a solution to a problem comes to you when you leave your desk and take a quick walk down the hall or around the block.

Stand Up When Anyone Walks into Your Office

Greeting visitors by leaping to your feet and warmly welcoming them not only gets you up and moving but also conveys enthusiasm and engagement and confers respect on your guest. Another advantage: In the case of unwelcome guests, standing up puts you in position to diplomatically put a hand on their shoulder and quickly guide them out of your office.

Relocate Commonly Used Items

One of the principles of conventional ergonomics is to keep commonly used items close at hand. From a productivity perspective, of course this makes sense. But do you really need a wastebasket, recycling bin, filing cabinet, and staple remover within arm's reach? Moving such items across the room can naturally add a fair amount of NEAT movement to your workday. Better yet, if your boss and co-workers are game, your whole office can share such items by centrally locating common supplies and equipment. Sustainability experts talk a lot about how we are moving to a sharing economy, and this would be a great way participate in that trend in your office.

Take the Stairs

Among the many laborsaving devices that have lead to our current movement-deprived lives are the elevators, escalators, and moving walkways that zip us around our offices and public spaces. Take the stairs instead. You sometimes have to look for them, and maybe even get a key or an access code, but there is almost always a publicly available stairwell as an alternative. Whether you're going up or down, stairways give you an opportunity to stretch your legs and get your blood flowing.

Some offices are better set up than others for this. For example, when the new office building that houses the Bullitt Foundation opened in Seattle recently, every news story mentioned the building's inviting stairways. The super-green building immediately attracted attention for its "irresistible stairway," which the Seattle Times reported, "rewards climbers with panoramic views of downtown and Puget Sound." The behavioral carrot aims to promote both health and energy conservation. The stick is a slow and less conveniently situated elevator that requires key card access. Even if your office stairway doesn't feature a view, you can motivate yourself by reflecting on the health benefits of taking the stairs as you go from floor to floor.

Get Off the Bus or Subway a Few Stops Early

If you take public transportation to work, you can start and end your day with some extra NEAT activity by getting off of the bus or subway a stop or two before your destination. Heck, if it's a really nice day, you can get off three or four stops early.

Park in the Far Corner of the Parking Lot

If you drive to work, instead of jockeying for the primo parking spot close to the door, park way out in the farthest corner of the parking lot.

Drink Lots of Water

Many doctors recommend that you drink at least eight cups of water a day to maintain a good level of hydration, (others dismiss this, saying that we get plenty of water from the food we eat, but there is little risk from drinking a bit more water than your body needs). You can fill a water bottle a couple of times a day and keep it at your desk, but to maximize the number of times you get up and get moving, I recommend using a smaller container to ensure regular refill trips to the water fountain or sink. Depending on your level of activity, the temperature and humidity in your office, and the size of your bladder, your water consumption will also prompt regular trips to the restroom — another opportunity to add a little gratuitous movement to your day.

Fidget, Squirm, and Stretch

In his early NEAT research, Levine discovered that people who simply fidget burn significantly more calories than truly sedentary people. In fact, this observation led to his exploration and development of the NEAT concept. Fidgeting, pacing, bending over to tie your shoes: these and many other seemingly trivial activities can add up to burn a significant number of calories throughout your workday.

Some evidence suggests that we are genetically predisposed to more or less fidgety behavior. If you find yourself naturally bopping up and down or pacing when you stand and fidgeting when you sit, you're probably one of the lucky ones predisposed to regular movement. If that's the case, then you can just ramp up your natural behavior a notch or two to boost your NEAT levels. If you find yourself comfortably slipping into stationary, sedentary patterns, then you may need to more proactively cultivate a few of these low-level activities.

Sitting on an Exercise Ball Doesn't Count

I know they're popular and fun, but I have to rain on the exercise-ball-as-desk-chair parade. There is no scientific evidence that sitting on an exercise ball engages any more muscles than sitting on a chair, so it's not a NEAT activity and doesn't belong on this list. I mention it here only because it's such a widespread practice.

None of the commonly mentioned hypotheses about sitting on an exercise ball have any scientific support. Your "core" is no more engaged than when you're sitting in a regular chair. Theoretically, the instability of the round surface causes your body to make constant small muscular adjustments, but real-time muscle measurements of exercise ball users show no evidence of this.

You slouch just as much, if not more, when sitting on an exercise ball than you do when sitting on a chair. In fact, one study even found evidence of spinal compression resulting from sitting on an exercise ball. Another study reported that the greater contact area on the soft surface of the exercise ball created discomfort for some study participants.

None of these studies showed exercise balls to be any worse than chairs, though, so if you enjoy sitting on one you're not putting yourself at any additional risk by continuing to sit on it. Just realize that you won't end up with a stronger core and six-pack abs.

Developing Routine Movement Habits

Add a Tiny Habit

Apply B.J. Fogg's recipe for a Tiny Habit: After I [existing habit/anchor], I will [new tiny behavior]. Some examples:

- After I pick up the phone, I will stand up for the duration of the call.
- After I check my email, I will stand up to read any messages that are more than one paragraph long.
- After I sit down at the weekly meeting, I will fidget as much as possible under the conference table (without disrupting the meeting or alarming my colleagues).
- After I walk into the lobby, I will enter the stairwell and walk up to my office (instead of taking the elevator).
- After I pull into the parking lot, I will find the parking spot farthest from the building entrance.
- After I complete a phone call, I will take a drink from my water bottle.

Modify a Habit Loop

Recall Charles Duhigg's habit loop and how you can hack it by identifying the routine, experimenting with the reward, isolating the cue, and planning how to implement your new habit loop. This is much more involved than a Tiny Habit, so you might want to review "Modify a Habit Loop" in Chapter 2 the first few times you go through this process. Here are a few ideas for identifying habits that can introduce more routine movement into your workday:

- Find an activity that you now do sitting down and modify the routine so that you do it standing up or moving around. Say, for example, that you always start your day by sitting down at your desk and reading through your email. That's the gist of the routine. The reward likely has something to do with productivity or simply knowing what's going on. The cue is likely either or both the time (start of the day) and the location (your desk). After experimenting with a few different rewards, it shouldn't be too hard to come up with a plan that shifts you from sitting to standing.
- If you regularly rendezvous with friends over coffee or a meal at the same time and place, play with this habit loop as a group to try to find ways to add more routine movement to your routine. You might discover, for example, that you could walk instead of driving to your destination, or you could find a coffee shop or cafe that has a counter where you can stand

while you eat, or you could add a gratuitous walk around the block after your gathering.

- Look at your commuting routine. How are you being rewarded now (time saved by driving instead of walking? increased comfort in your own car versus public transportation? able to sleep an extra 15 minutes by driving rather than taking the bus?). The cue for this loop is probably tied to the time that you're expected to arrive at work. Can you find a way to modify this habit loop to walk all or part of the way to your office? If you can't walk all the way to work, can you get off the bus or subway one or more stops early?

- Identify some routine interactions with colleagues that you now do by email or phone. Could you walk to your colleague's office instead of communicating electronically? Could any of these routines fit into a walking meeting?

- What's your routine for breaking through a creative block as a deadline looms? If your tendency is to glue yourself to your desk and grind through the process, you might want to experiment with taking a 10- or 15-minute walk instead. You have probably experienced sudden clarity by simply stepping back from a project and taking a walk around the block. There is plenty of scientific evidence to support this practice. A recent Stanford study (Oppezzo & Schwartz 2014) found, for example, that creative output increases by about 60% when walking. So dissect deadline-pressure habit loops and look for ways to add a quick walk to them.

Adopt a Practice

Try some of these practices that naturally encourage routine movement:

- In the software-development world, daily "stand-up" meetings encourage quick check-ins and updates from team members. If you're involved in a regular meeting that typically lasts less than 15 minutes, propose that you meet standing up.

- Wear a pedometer or other activity tracker. Simply tracking your daily movement activity can push you on your way to getting the optimal 10,000 steps per day of routine movement.

- Tai chi's slow, specific movements are easy to subtly and unobtrusively include into my workday routines. It's easier to do this if you work at a standing desk, of course, but you can also work it in whenever you have the chance to stand up. Practices like yoga and Pilates also give you a palette of movements that you can work into your office day.
- If you work at home, get a dog. You'll be out for a nice walk at least a couple of times a day.

Take a Plunge

Go nuts! Throw a monkey wrench into your current set-up to create big, instant change that gets you up and moving. A few ideas:

- Make a simple standing desk by elevating your current desk on cinder blocks, bed risers, or PVC tubing. Or simply put a cardboard box on top of your desk and set your laptop on it.
- Or you can buy a commercial standing desk, ideally a height-adjustable one so that you can easily change positions throughout the day.
- Splurge on a Stir Kinetic Desk. This nifty, new, automatically height-adjustable desk costs a fortune (almost $4,000), but it looks great and it cleverly reminds you to stay active during your workday.
- Buy a treadmill desk. Or make one from the old treadmill languishing in your garage. You don't have to walk on your treadmill all day, of course; even a few bouts of walking while working can help.
- Team up with your colleagues and persuade your boss to buy a shared treadmill workstation.
- Make or buy a bicycle desk. Some models now even let you power your laptop with your pedaling.
- If you live in the suburbs, move to the city. City dwellers naturally walk and move more throughout the day, burning significantly more calories than car-bound suburbanites.
- Change careers. Follow your dream of becoming a chef or a flight attendant. Turn your backyard hobby into a career as a carpenter or stonemason. Go to massage school or become a personal trainer. Teach ballroom dancing or guide rafting trips. Plenty of fine ways to make a living don't involve

working at a desk all day and do involve a lot of natural all-day movement.

Suggested Reading

Nano Workouts: Get in Shape and Lose Weight During Everyday Activities, Joakim Christoffersson

Get Up!: Why Your Chair Is Killing You and What You Can Do About It, James Levine

Move a Little, Lose a Lot: New NEAT Science Reveals How to Be Thinner, Happier, and Smarter, James Levine and Selene Yeager

Sitting Kills, Moving Heals: How Everyday Movement Will Prevent Pain, Illness, and Early Death – and Exercise Alone Won't, Joan Vernikos

Sources

"Ultragreen Building Is Ready for Challenge." The Seattle Times. April 26, 2014.

Gregory, Diane E., Nadine M. Dunk, and Jack P. Callaghan. "Stability Ball Versus Office Chair: Comparison of Muscle Activation and Lumbar Spine Posture During Prolonged Sitting." Human Factors 48, no. 1 (Spring 2006): 142–53.

Jackson, J. A., P. Banerjee-Guenette, D. E. Gregory, and J. P. Callaghan. "Should We Be More on the Ball?: The Efficacy of Accommodation Training on Lumbar Spine Posture, Muscle Activity, and Perceived Discomfort During Stability Ball Sitting." Human Factors: The Journal of the Human Factors and Ergonomics Society 55, no. 6 (December 1, 2013): 1064–76.

Levine, James A., Sara J. Schleusner, and Michael D. Jensen. "Energy Expenditure of Nonexercise Activity." The American Journal of Clinical Nutrition 72, no. 6 (December 1, 2000): 1451–54.

Levine, James, and Selene Yeager. Move a Little, Lose a Lot: New NEAT Science Reveals How to Be Thinner, Happier, and Smarter. New York: Crown Publishers, 2009.

Oppezzo, Marily, and Daniel L. Schwartz. "Give Your Ideas Some Legs: The Positive Effect of Walking on Creative Thinking." Journal of Experimental Psychology: Learning, Memory, and Cognition, 2014.

Tikkanen, Olli, Piia Haakana, Arto J. Pesola, Keijo Häkkinen, Timo Rantalainen, Marko Havu, Teemu Pullinen, and Taija Finni. "Muscle Activity and Inactivity Periods during Normal Daily Life." PLoS ONE 8, no. 1 (January 18, 2013): e52228.

Vernikos, Joan. Sitting Kills, Moving Heals: How Everyday Movement Will Prevent Pain, Illness, and Early Death – and Exercise Alone Won't. 1 edition. Fresno, Calif: Quill Driver Books, 2011.

This is a partial list of sources consulted as I wrote this chapter, including only items mentioned or referred to. For a full list of everything I read as I prepared this chapter, please visit sitless.com/chapter3

Chapter 4
Office Ergonomics

Sitting disease can take decades to manifest. The pain and injury that result from a poor ergonomic set-up can appear much faster.

Whether you're sitting down, standing up, or walking at your desk, you want to be comfortable and productive and safe from injury. Just as athletes prevent injuries and perform best with the right gear, the right office equipment set up in the right way can prevent pain and support you in your work.

The U.S. Occupational Safety & Health Administration (OSHA) and similar agencies in other countries urge employers to train their employees in ergonomics and to help their workers recognize early symptoms of office-work injuries. When it comes to real-life, day-to-day practice, most office workers are on their own.

Even if you work in an organization that offers ergonomic support, the typical office intervention is a one-time event — part of the ritual of accepting a new job, moving to a new office, or getting a new desk. You may get some assistance if your doctor prescribes it and if you push the bureaucracy. That may be a special chair or a standing desk or a keyboard. If you are lucky enough to work in an organization with good resources, the "ergonomics person" might also recommend a gadget or two and give you some training on how to set up your workstation. And typically that is that. As soon as the expert leaves, you are on your own.

You use your office equipment all day, every day. So it makes sense to pay ongoing attention to it. Because most offices offer no ongoing ergonomic evaluation process, it behooves you to understand some basic ergonomic principles and how to apply them at your desk, day-to-day, hour-to-hour. This chapter is a crash course in developing some good ergonomics self-assessment habits.

Principles of Ergonomics

The overarching goal of ergonomics is to balance comfort and productivity. Ideally, every physical feature in your office, from the layout and lighting to the controls of the latest electronic device on your desk, should support this goal.

Modern office ergonomics grew out of the worlds of manufacturing, engineering, and computing. The ergonomics principles developed in those disciplines lay the foundation for your relationship with your office equipment.

Put Your Body in a Neutral Posture

Your office equipment should allow you to position your body to honor its natural shapes and contours. Your spine should retain its natural, gentle "S" shape, from the base of your spine all the way up to your head. Your joints should be in positions as neutral as possible, with no excessive flexion or extension or twisting or bending. Your arms should hang naturally from your shoulders, your elbows at your side. Your wrists should be relaxed, your hand in the same plane as your forearm, with your forearms parallel to your work surface. Your eyes should be level with the horizon and your chin tucked in. As you'll see, you can maintain this neutral posture while using any of your office equipment.

Don't Reach

Keep your work close to your body. Whether you're lifting a heavy box of paper or typing a short email, keeping your gear close to your body reduces strain and keeps you from stretching your body into contorted positions.

Keep Your Work at the Proper Height

This is a variation of the "no reaching" principle. Your chair, desk, computer, and other gear should always be positioned at a height that matches your body.

Reduce Pressure Points

You can't avoid pressing your fingers into your keyboard, and your butt is going to press into your chair whenever you sit down. But you want to avoid unnecessary pressure points. This doesn't mean that you can't comfortably support yourself. For example, a padded wrist rest can help keep your wrists in a neutral position as you type. But when your office equipment presses on your body in a less supportive way, you've gone from support to pressure. Classic pressure spots are at the wrist if you are resting your forearms directly on the desk surface or on the edge of your desk, and at the back of the legs if your chair's seat pan has a high front edge.

Minimize Fatigue and Static Load

This principle comes straight from the manufacturing setting, the source of most ergonomic principles. On an assembly line, holding heavy tools for hours on end would obviously wear you out. In the office, the less-obvious hazard micro-fatigue because your leg muscles have been removed from the postural support system that holds you upright in your chair. Taking regular standing breaks can reduce this fatigue. If you use a standing workstation, the static load on your legs and hips can cause knee and low-back pain, which you can reduce by simply elevating one foot on a small stool or other footrest.

Avoid Excessive Motion

This principle also goes back to manufacturing settings, which highly value efficiency. Applied in the office, it is related to the "no reaching" principle. One of my massage clients provides a good example. She spent a couple of months in a temporary office, where her scanner, which she used repeatedly throughout the day, was on the left side of her desk. She is right handed. So every time she used the scanner she had to awkwardly reach across her body to load documents into it. To keep excessive motion to a minimum, position commonly used tools and equipment where you can reach them gracefully and effortlessly. (This principle sometimes seems to conflict with the advice on routine movement in Chapter 3. But unnecessary excessive motion caused by a poor ergonomic set-up differs significantly from the gratuitous movement you intentionally introduce to combat sitting disease.

Pay Attention to Details

Little things add up, especially when you do them all day. A small movement or postural distortion that might not matter if you did it for 10 or 15 minutes can leave you injured and in pain if you do it for hours on end. For example, even a small amount of reaching out for your mouse can eventually pull your shoulder forward and down, resulting in nervy pain in your arms and hands. And even the slightest up tilt of your head to peer into a poorly positioned computer monitor can leave you with headaches and a sore neck.

Take Regular Breaks

At the very least, stand up on a regular basis to disrupt the pathological effects of sitting disease. From an orthopedic perspective, it's also important to regularly disrupt your repetitive work patterns and use your body in a different way.

Maintain a Comfortable Work Environment

A pleasant workspace enhances the effect of your physical positioning and body support. So pay attention to your physical environment. Cultivate a houseplant or two and/or arrange for a glimpse of nature outside your window. Make sure the office lighting illuminates your work area without creating glare on your computer screen. Good ventilation and heating and cooling systems support your comfort in the office, while a drafty office or an air conditioning system that chills the workplace can make you squirm and reach for a sweater. For some, a quiet environment lets you focus on your work; for those who crave stimulation, silence may be stultifying. A noisy office can be invigorating but when you need to focus can be distracting. Be aware of your environmental factors and manage them the best you can.

Now let's apply those principles to each of your office accouterments, starting with your chair — where sitting disease begins.

Chair Ergonomics

Traditionally, office workers begin their days by plopping down in a chair. At this point, I'm sure I need not remind you that you should be in your chair as little as possible during your workday. For those rare occasions when you are sitting, be sure to apply these ergonomic principles.

Neutral Posture

Your chair should help you maintain a neutral posture. This means keeping your pelvis in neutral with respect to your spine and letting your spine naturally rise up out of your pelvis, much as it does when you're standing.

The best way to get a feel for this neutral posture is to use a chair that has a relatively firm and minimally padded seat pan so that you can feel your "sits bones," the knobby protuberances at the base of your pelvis (anatomically known as the ischial tuberosities). Using your sits bones as a fulcrum, you can gently rock your pelvis forward and back, while doing your best to keep your spine straight up and down. If you tilt all the way back you'll feel your tailbone tuck under you (trust me, you don't want to sit like that all day, though many slouchers do). If you tilt all the way forward, you'll exaggerate (perhaps painfully) the slight forward curve in your low back. Your chair should let you sit comfortably in the middle of this forward-to-back range.

You can double-check your pelvis-spine neutrality by placing your hands palm-side down on your low back, with your forefingers across the top of your hip bones. This lets your fingertips feel the curve in your low back, which should be a very shallow C-shaped dip. As you tuck your tailbone under you and tilt your pelvis back, you'll feel your lower back straighten out. As you roll your pelvis forward, you'll exaggerate the forward curve in your low back. Make sure that your chair lets you sit comfortably in the middle of this forward-to-back range with just a little natural forward C-shaped curve in the lower spine between the top of your hips and bottom of your ribcage.

One sure way to ruin your neutral sitting posture is to have to reach awkwardly for items that aren't close at hand. A chair with well-lubricated wheels and a floor surface that permits easy rolling can help you stay in a neutral posture, even when you're moving just a short distance.

Lumbar Support

Many modern office chairs include lumbar support, which is intended to help you maintain this neutral posture. If you use a chair with lumbar support, or if you add a lumbar roll to your existing chair, the shape of the support should conform with the shape of your lower back, curving slightly forward with the curve conforming to your back in its neutral position. Some lumbar rolls, like the popular McKenzie model, are as much as six inches in diameter, pushing your low back too far forward. For most people, a better choice is a two- to three-inch-thick lumbar support pad that curves to conform to your natural lumbar shape. (On the other hand, if you are stuck in an airline or car seat or chair that has a negative curve at your low back, you may need one of those thicker rolls.)

Another way to keep your lumbar spine in neutral is to try to mimic standing posture even as you sit. That's the idea behind office furniture like the Balans kneeling chair. These chairs have a forward-sloped seat pan and backward-sloping shin rest, letting your knees drop down and opening the angle between your thighs and your back. Theoretically, opening up the thigh-spine angle re-engages low-back muscles as if you were standing, but muscle activity measurements haven't entirely supported that theory. Nevertheless, many people find those chairs comfortable, and I can attest from years of using a Balans-style chair that they engage your body in a different way. The kneeling position is a nice break from sitting in a conventional chair or standing up for long stretches. Like exercise-ball chairs, though, the Balans-style can encourage slouching and strain your spine, so I wouldn't sit on one all day.

Saddle seats and perching stools like the Back App chair also let your knees drop down below your hips as you sit. Unlike kneeling models, these chairs let you keep your feet on the floor as you sit, making them popular with hairdressers, dental hygienists, and others who need to move around easily. In the office, such chairs work best with a sit-stand desk adjusted to a height that lets you perch halfway between sitting and standing. In the perching position — which looks a lot like "horse stance" in the martial arts or the way a linebacker crouches as the ball is about to be snapped — your leg and low-back muscles are more engaged and it's almost impossible to slouch.

Gadgets like the Nada "Back-Up" support your lumbar spine with a padded belt that goes across your low back and encircles your knees as you sit, letting you sit comfortably with practically no effort. Muscle activity measurements show that these contraptions offer the most support, meaning that the muscles in your low back are least engaged when using them. In terms of comfort and rest, this is an obvious benefit. So if you are forced to sit at work and are having low-back pain, those gizmos can help you get through the day. But because they almost completely turn off muscle activity, they could be an "inactivity physiology" culprit.

Scientists have examined how each type of chair and lumbar support affects your body. Their studies have shown that perching requires a fair amount of muscle activity, kneeling chairs and exercise balls a bit less, regular sitting even less, and "Back Up" and similar devices almost no muscle activity. A number of studies have surveyed sitters about their perceptions of the comfort of each sitting arrangement. Not surprisingly, most people perceive the least engaged positions as the most comfortable.

Posture guru Esther Gokhale provides at least one more approach to lumbar support. She designed the "Gokhale Pain Free Chair" that, instead of supporting the low back, lifts the trunk up and away from the pelvis. Her design aligns with a practice she teaches called "stretchsitting," which involves draping your torso over the back of your chair to elongate the lumbar spine. You'll learn more about Gokhale in the next chapter on posture.

No Reaching & Proper Height

The main application of the no reaching and proper height principles when you are sitting means that you shouldn't have to reach for the floor with your feet. Adjust your seat height so that your feet rest firmly and comfortably on the floor. If your chair won't adjust low enough to let your feet rest on the floor, don't let your legs dangle; use a footrest to support them.

No Pressure Points

Applying the no-pressure-points principle to sitting involves your legs, arms, buttocks, and low back — the parts of your body that make contact with your chair. Obviously, you can't eliminate pressure points when you sit, but you can manage them.

Your chair's seat should be only minimally padded. Most of us have plenty of padding in our butts anyway. More importantly, to get into a neutral posture when you're sitting, you need to feel your "sits bones," not have them disappear into a plushly padded seat. To control a position of your pelvis that supports a neutral posture, you have to be able to push back against something. When your butt has disappeared into a fluffy cushion your chair gives you little kinesthetic feedback about your position.

Many office chairs are designed with an upward lip at the front edge of the chair. This design unnecessarily compresses your hamstrings, the long muscles on the back of your legs that run from your hips to your knees. You should be able to adjust your chair to minimize this pressure, first by lifting the back of the seat pan so that your hips are higher than your knees. It's also ideal to have a "waterfall" design, a slight downward curved slope at the front edge of the seat pan to reduce pressure on the back of your knee joint. Your chair's seat pan should also leave an inch or two of room between the front edge of the seat pan and the back of your knee.

Most ergonomists recommend against arm rests. They can easily go from supporting your forearms to putting pressure on them. If you do use arm rests, they should have rounded edges and be made of a soft material. They should let your arms hang comfortably at your side, neither pressing them up so your shoulders are elevated nor pushing them out so your arms are away from your body. If you can't remove your chair's arm rests, adjust them to their lowest position to keep them out of your way.

Pay Attention to Details

Regardless of the style of chair you sit in, you will benefit from learning all of the possible adjustments you can make. If you sit in a conventional chair, at the very least you should be able to adjust the seat height so that your feet rest comfortably on the floor (or a footrest) and to adjust the tilt of the seat pan so that you can position your hips a little higher than your knees. The best chairs let you make many more adjustments – tilt, tilt tension, arm-rest height and width, as well as the amount of lumbar support. If you don't have the instruction manual for your chair, try doing a search at YouTube. Both manufacturers and users have uploaded hundreds of instructional videos that show you how to operate almost any modern office chair. Your office chair should, of course, be sturdy and safe. This means a five-arm base and sturdy casters that let you roll smoothly on the floor surface.

Regular breaks

I'm sure you need no reminder at this point that if there's any one place in your office from which you definitely need regular breaks, it's your chair. In fact, if you're in a chair right now, stand up and stretch your legs a bit.

Desk Ergonomics

In a perfect ergonomic world, your desk would be shaped like a kidney bean, with you at the inside apex of the curve and all of your gadgets within easy reach. In our world of traditional right-angle office furniture, though, most us will be walking, standing, perching, or (occasionally) sitting at a rectangular desk.

Neutral Posture & No Reaching

Regardless of the shape of your desk, there should be plenty of room for your stuff. Traditionally, ergonomics experts recommend a desk with a continuous, flat work surface that is large enough for the stuff you routinely use and that keeps frequently used items close at hand. Keeping your most commonly used items close to you minimizes awkward postures and reduces unnecessary, repetitive exertions that can lead to injuries.

(These repetitive exertions are different, of course, from the gratuitously introduced routine movements suggested in Chapter 3. Occasionally getting up to walk across the room to the printer is much different from repeatedly reaching across your desk to a scan documents.)

You've probably already got your desk organized in a way that suits your work. It's still a good idea to review your set-up once in a while to make sure that you aren't compromising your posture or reaching for routinely used items. While a proactive review is preferred, it is often a new muscle ache or tension pattern that impels you to re-examine your ergonomic situation. Whatever prompts your review, make sure that you can reach all of your routinely used items — from your coffee cup to your keyboard — without reaching out too far with your arms or compromising your neutral posture.

Proper Height & No Pressure Points

Adjust your desk surface to a height that lets your legs slide under the desktop without hitting the desk surface, keyboard tray, or other obstacle. No sharp edges or protruding parts should be able to hit your legs as you swivel in your chair.

Pay Attention to Details

If you keep your computer CPU box or other large items under your desk, make sure that they are out of the way of your feet and legs. Control clutter and use cable organizers to keep the wiring from brushing against your legs. If you find yourself bumping into sharp edges, pad the edge of your desk with an inexpensive material such as pipe insulation.

Standing Desk Ergonomics

Standing at the office is a great alternative to sitting all day. When you are standing, you burn more calories, your cholesterol levels stabilize, and your body better supports your low back and more easily finds a neutral posture. There are some problems with standing — increased risk of varicose veins being perhaps the most troublesome, along with some very manageable musculoskeletal discomfort. But these hazards are well known from the ergonomics experiences of generations of highway toll-takers, chefs, hairdressers, grocery store checkout clerks, assembly-line workers, and others who must be on their feet for hours at a time. A number of proven ergonomics practices can address these issues.

Although standing is great, it is not the be-all and end-all of good office ergonomics. Remember, if the overarching hypothesis of this book is correct, the most important thing you can do is move more at work. You can do that by incorporating as much routine physical activity as possible into your workday and by varying your position as often as possible. The ideal ergonomic set-up would support and encourage this by incorporating a sit-stand height-adjustable desk accompanied by a height-adjustable perching chair and a low-profile treadmill so that you can walk while you work for part of the day.

The availability and variety of standing workstations has expanded dramatically since I began research for this book in 2008. Hundreds of do-it-yourself standing desk projects are now documented on YouTube and around the web. You can see hundreds more furniture mash-ups at websites like IkeaHackers.net. Commercially available standing desk options now range from fancy sit-stand executive models that cost thousands of dollars to student models at bargain prices.

Whichever standing desk you wind up with, here are a number of ways to apply the principles of ergonomics and optimize your workstation for standing.

Neutral Posture

Neutral posture is easy to attain when you stand. Our ability to effortlessly stand upright for hours on end is unique to humans. It's the adaptation that frees our hands to use tools and lets us see more of our world than we would on all fours. Your body is well suited to regular standing.

No Reaching

You should be able to reach your commonly used stuff as easily when standing as when sitting. This seems obvious, but I mention it mainly because many of the standing desks I've seen have had much smaller work surfaces than conventional desks. Both commercial and do-it-yourself designs often repurpose shelving or other furniture (bookcases, for example) that isn't designed to be used as desktops. If you normally keep a lot of stuff on your desktop, don't scrimp when you switch to a standing desk. Keeping all of your commonly used materials close at hand is just as important when you're standing. On the other hand, many computer-centric office jobs these days can be conducted almost entirely using only a computer and a phone; a smaller desktop can work just fine for those jobs.

Proper Height

The relationship between your upper body and your office equipment should be the same whether you are sitting, standing, or perched somewhere in between. A fixed-height standing desk can work OK (I wrote about 90% of this book at one), but an adjustable-height desk is ideal. Height adjustability permits both sitting and standing, as well as alternative positions like kneeling and perching, making it easier for you to change positions throughout your workday.

No Pressure Points

When you're standing, the main pressure points are, of course, on the bottoms of your feet. Wearing comfortable shoes that let your toes spread out can relieve the pressure on the sides of your feet that stylish shoes can inflict. Because my office is next door to the flagship Nordstrom store and many of its employees are my massage clients, I am particularly attuned to discomfort caused by narrow high-heeled shoes. Ladies (and any high-heel-wearing men out there), when you use a standing desk, please slip on a pair of comfortable flats or sneakers while standing at your desk.

Using a padded anti-fatigue mat can further soften the pressure on the soles of your feet. If you dislike the industrial look of commercial anti-fatigue mats, new padded bathroom mats are available in a variety of styles and colors. To add some variety to your standing day, consider keeping one or two extra mats around, each with a slightly different texture and padding. If you work at home (or have a very supportive workplace), you could even stand barefoot in a small heated sandbox, scrunching the warm sand between your toes all day.

Minimize Fatigue and Static Load

Standing in one position for an extended period can irritate your body's supporting musculoskeletal systems, particularly your knees and low back. You can tame this pain by alternately elevating one foot at a time, using a footrest, an old shipping box, or any other sturdy bar-rail-height gadget that can lift your foot 8 or 10 inches.

Much of the discomfort that comes with standing is caused by its static nature, so simply moving a bit and changing positions frequently can break the anatomical patterns that cause the pain. I stand at my desk almost all of the time now, but I am rarely still. I walk in place, do simple dance steps and shallow lunges, and sink into a perching position when I'm reading instead of typing. A recently introduced height-adjustable desk, the Stir Kinetic Desk, includes a computerized reminder system that encourages this kind of routine movement.

Pay Attention to Details

Your exposure to lighting glare, steamy or icy blasts from heating and air conditioning vents, and even noise levels may change as you move from sitting to standing. This is unlikely, of course, but paying attention to these little details can help maintain your overall comfort level at work.

Make sure the standing desk you choose is sturdy and safe. Many manufactured and homemade standing desks fail to account for the instability that comes with a taller structure. Simply lengthening the desk legs doesn't get the job done. A good standing desk design includes cross-bracing and sturdy components that keep your desk from wobbling.

Regular breaks

Do not stand — or sit or kneel or adopt any other one position — all day. With an ideal workstation, you can move effortlessly from standing to sitting (or to some other favorite desk posture). Whether you work at a fixed-height or a fancy multiposition workstation, you can and should take regular breaks from standing. I take mini exercise breaks from my standing desk several times an hour to do 5 or 10 deep knee bends, a few tai chi moves, or some chest- and shoulder-opening stretches.

Treadmill Desk Ergonomics

Treadmill desks are a fantastic way to add routine movement to your workday. You stroll at a leisurely, non-exercise pace (typically between one and two miles per hour) as you work at a standing-style workstation. The treadmill surface is typically lower-profile and geared differently than an exercise treadmill, so you don't feel like you're at the gym.

Research has demonstrated that productivity is only slightly impaired by working at a treadmill desk, and then only for projects that required precise hand motions. If your work — graphic design, for example — requires fine motor control, it may be affected a bit (which makes sense if you think about the natural arm swing that comes with walking). But you can type, read, and perform most other common office activities on a treadmill desk with little or no ill effect.

All of the same ergonomic concerns that apply to a standing desk apply to a treadmill desk. The main difference between standing and walking, of course, is that you're moving, which introduces a few biomechanical considerations as well as some safety concerns.

Neutral Posture

Walking is even more natural than standing, so it's easy to maintain a neutral posture walking at a treadmill desk.

No Reaching

The same principles apply as for sitting and standing: keep everything within easy reach. One consideration unique to treadmill desks is the position of the desk surface relative to the treadmill's walking surface. Make sure that your desk surface is positioned in a way that lets you walk normally without banging your feet into the machine's motor casing. When you first set up a treadmill desk, make sure that you have room to move the desktop far enough toward your position on the treadmill so that you can take normal, natural strides while still reaching your equipment without kicking the motor casing.

Proper Height

Your desktop should be at a comfortable height that lets you reach all of your gear easily and allows room for your legs to swing naturally as you walk without hitting any part of the desk or treadmill — the same principles that apply to sitting and standing.

Treadmill desks are designed to move very slowly, just enough to keep your legs moving. Still, if you favor the higher end of the treadmill speed range, you may feel some fatigue after a long stretch of walking at work. If you begin to tire, take a standing or sitting break or simply reduce the speed.

Pay Attention to Details

Just as you would with a standing desk, make sure the desk part of your treadmill workstation is sturdy enough for its height. This is, of course, even more important when you are moving at your desk, especially if you lean your forearms on your desk as you walk. Ensure that your desk surface is sturdy and safe.

Some users have reported issues with static electricity as they walk on a treadmill desk. This problem is more common if your treadmill is on a carpeted floor, but it can even happen on wood and other floor surfaces. There is little risk to you or your colleagues from an occasional mild shock, but static electricity can definitely affect your computer.

You can take a number of measures to overcome a static electricity problem in your office. The first thing to do is to ground both the treadmill and your computer with three-prong plugs in a properly grounded outlet. To keep your computer physically separate from you and your desk, you can use a wireless Bluetooth keyboard and mouse. An anti-static rubber mat can isolate your treadmill from the floor (while simultaneously protecting the floor from dings and other damage).

If you re-use an exercise treadmill to make your own treadmill desk, make sure that you leave the tilt angle flat and always walk at a slow, non-exercise speed. Some exercise treadmills can be a bit noisy. If you or your colleagues are concerned about treadmill noise, you can get one designed specifically for office use. If the source of the noise is your shoes clomping on the treadmill, you can try shoes with a softer sole.

Computer Ergonomics

Computing has evolved considerably since the introduction of the IBM PC 30 years ago. The evolution has accelerated recently, with the increasing popularity of laptops over desktop computers and the rapid adoption of tablets, smartphones, and other portable computing devices. In early 2014, the research firm Canalys reported that 50% of personal computer sales are now tablets, 33% are laptops, and only 17% are desktops. Granted, many of those tablets are used at home, and many of those laptops are used by students, but the trend toward using a variety of different and increasingly portable computers is definitely taking hold in the office.

Depending on your job and the industry you work in, you are likely to be using something other than a desktop computer much of the time. Yet, most of the ergonomic advice in circulation assumes that you work at a desktop computer. This is one of the reasons for my principles-based approach to ergonomics. As we look at each component of your computer you will see how ergonomics principles can help you adapt to the ever-changing computing environment.

Computer Keyboard Ergonomics

Over the past 30 years, as personal computers grew from novelty to ubiquity, we have all become typists and data-entry clerks. Back when typists used manual and electric typewriters, injuries from such work were relatively rare. Within a decade after the introduction of the personal computer, workers compensation claims for repetitive strain injuries related to keyboard use exploded, and even folks who didn't file claims were beginning to feel the pain of modern keyboard work.

So what changed? Why do computer keyboards cause so many more injuries than typewriters did?

First, many more people are typing now. Typewriters and data-entry consoles used to be confined to secretaries' desks, typing pools, and computing rooms. Now no one outside of the executive suite has a secretary, while at the same time our information-heavy jobs require much more writing, analysis, reporting, programming, and other typing-intensive tasks.

Second, manual typewriters, and even electric typewriters, involved more body movements, using the whole arm and a variety of muscles, which spread the burden of the movement across more anatomical structures. Modern computer keyboards are designed to require as little movement as possible, so a few structures — the fingers, wrists, and forearms mostly — do all of the work. Modern low-profile keyboards on laptops and desktops also make you reach for the keyboard differently, contorting your forearms into uncomfortable positions. Increasingly compact keyboards bring your wrists closer and closer together, causing you to bend your wrists to line up your fingers with the keyboard ("ulnar deviation" in medical parlance), putting you at risk for carpal tunnel syndrome and other repetitive-strain injuries.

Third, old-fashioned typewriters weren't inextricably linked to a typing and computing system. The whole computer arrangement (peering into your monitor and reaching out for your mouse and keyboard) promotes the notorious forward-shoulder office posture, which can result in impingement of the nerves and blood vessels that go into the arm and hands. In fact, much of the pain, tingling, numbness, and lethargy that you feel in your arms and hands is actually due to constrictions way up in your chest, shoulders, and neck that ensue from this posture.

Finally, modern typing is awkward by design. The familiar QWERTY keyboard layout (named for the first six keys in the upper-left of the keyboard) was actually designed to slow down typists. Early manual typewriters frequently jammed as typists got the hang of the layout and began typing faster than the machine could handle. Despite the typists' speed, the jams actually slowed down production, so it made sense at the time to throttle back their flying fingers so that they wouldn't send multiple typebars smashing to the paper at the same time. That relic of the manual-typewriter age now makes typing more awkward than it needs to be.

Here's how to apply ergonomics principles to your keyboard use.

Neutral Posture

Your keyboard set-up should let you work with your wrists in a relaxed, straight, neutral position. Look at your wrists as you type. Looking from the top, can you draw a straight line from the midline of your forearm to the first segment of your middle finger? If not, your hand has deviated from its neutral side-to-side range, causing stress at your wrist. Looking from the side, can you draw a straight line from the side of your forearm through middle of the Y formed by your relaxed thumb and index finger? If not, your wrist is in flexion or extension. Working from the neutral position between both the side-to-side and flexion and extension ranges is the key to preventing carpal tunnel syndrome and other repetitive strain injuries.

Keep your forearms, arms, and shoulders in a neutral position. Place your keyboard so that you can easily reach all the keys with your shoulder blades retracted (pulled back toward the midline), with your upper arms hanging easily straight down at your side, and with your forearms lined up parallel with the surface of your keyboard. If your keyboard is flat and on a flat surface, then your forearms should be roughly parallel to the floor. If your keyboard slopes upward away from you, then your elbows should be a bit below the front edge of the keyboard to keep your forearms parallel to the keypad. Similarly, if your keyboard slopes down and away from you, your elbows should be a bit above the front edge of your keyboard.

No Reaching

You shouldn't have to reach for your keyboard. Positioning your keyboard so that it draws your hands and arms even just a few inches forward pulls your upper arms and shoulders forward, starting a pattern that eventually leads to the classic "office slump." Instead, position your keyboard so that you can comfortably reach the main row of keys while keeping your upper arms hanging vertically at your side, with your upper arms resting against your torso.

Neither should you have to reach side-to-side as you work at your keyboard. Many modern office keyboards include a numeric keypad, typically on the right side of the keyboard. If you center the whole keyboard in front of you, you'll end up constantly reaching to the left. Instead, place your keyboard so that the key for the letter "B" lines up with your body's midline.

Proper Height

Your keyboard should be positioned so that it is approximately level with your elbows when your arms are hanging naturally at your side. For most desks, the best way to hold your keyboard to achieve this height is to use a keyboard tray that hangs under the front edge of your desk surface. The tray should be wide enough to accommodate both your keyboard and mouse. If you have a numeric keypad on your keyboard, this means you'll probably need a tray that's at least 24 inches wide, and ideally a little wider. Many, if not most, keyboard trays are narrower than this. Keyboard tray designers seem to favor a narrow profile, so you may need to shop around for a tray that is wide enough. As of this writing Kensington was producing a 26-inch-wide model and ItalModern a chic-looking 30-inch-wide model. Regardless of the exact width of your tray, make sure that you can position your keyboard tray so that the letter "B" on the keyboard lines up with the middle of your torso, as discussed above.

Some keyboard trays are mounted on a height-adjustable swing arm. These arms also move forward and back as they adjust up and down. Make sure you account for this front-to-back movement as you position your keyboard tray in relation to your chair and monitor.

No Pressure Points & Minimize Static Load

If you have positioned your keyboard at the correct angle, height, and distance for your body, you are unlikely to experience undue pressure on your arms, wrists, or hands. If you do feel pressure, reevaluate your arrangement and see if you can make adjustments that reduce or eliminate it.

After you are satisfied with the angle at which your hands and forearms approach your keyboard, if you still feel like you have to work at it to keep your arms and hands comfortably positioned over your keyboard, you may want to use a wrist support. If you use a wrist rest, make sure that it is supportive enough to comfortably hold your wrists in line with your keyboard and soft enough to feel comfortable against your wrists. Your wrists should feel supported but not compressed. Many wrist rests are made of somewhat exotic materials, so if you have any allergies, be sure to carefully examine the list of materials before buying.

No Excessive Motion

When it comes to typing, the surest way to eliminate unnecessary motion is to learn to touch type. This skill not only distributes your typing effort across all of your digits, it also keeps you from having to constantly look down at the keyboard, helping you avoid neck strain as your head bobs up and down.

On the other hand, looking at the world through an office-fitness filter, always looking for ways to add gratuitous NEAT movement into your workday, you may ask if there's a way to re-introduce old-fashioned, less-painful, manual typing to the modern office. Indeed there is. The USB Typewriter company helps you convert your old manual typewriter into a modern keyboard input device with a do-it-yourself kit, or you can buy a typewriter that they have already converted for you. I don't know how NEAT this actually is, but I can guarantee that it would be a lot of fun.

Alternative Keyboard Styles

Most of us still use standard-issue flat keyboards that come with our computers or on our laptops, but a number of ergonomically more friendly keyboards are available.

You have likely seen the fancy "ergonomic" keyboards made by Microsoft and other manufacturers. These keyboards split the key surface in half and raise it in the middle so that your keyboard looks a bit like a small tent. This keeps you from having to rotate your hands all the way down to a flat position, reducing pressure on your wrists and forearms.

Many other alternative keyboard designs are available. Some slightly angle the keys themselves. Some split the keyboard while keeping the conventional straight layout to reduce your need to pronate (to turn your palm downward) your wrists. Some models, notably those from Kinesis, have little keyboard wells designed to minimize the need to reach for the keys. Some completely split the keyboard so that you can line up each half directly in front of each of your arms. There are even split keyboards that are completely vertical so that you interact with your keyboard more like an accordion player than a typist. A massage client of mine once cut a conventional keyboard in half and hung it over his chair like saddlebags so that he could type with his arms hanging straight down at his side.

All of these designs make sense, in that they attempt to reduce unnecessary pronation, ulnar deviation, and wrist flexion or extension. Many people report more comfort when they use these alternatives. No extensive research supports one option over another, so I urge you to experiment and explore to find the right alternative for you.

One other alternative is available: The Dvorak keyboard layout was designed to undo the deliberate obstacles of the QWERTY layout. A Dvorak keyboard places the most commonly used letters on the middle row of keys under your strongest fingers and is laid out so that common letter combinations alternate between hands. This lets you type using less finger motion, reduces errors, and can increase your typing speed. Most modern computers let you change your keyboard to the Dvorak layout. Because of the steep learning curve, however, few people actually use it. Still, if you are just getting started with typing or you have the patience to re-learn touch typing, the Dvorak layout is worth exploring.

Regular breaks

Operating a keyboard is one of the leading causes of repetitive strain injuries in the office, so it is particularly important to take regular breaks from typing and data entry. Try to alternate between typing and other tasks as much as possible, and take regular breaks to stand up and stretch out your wrists and forearms. Even better, you can eliminate typing almost entirely with Dragon Dictate and similar voice-recognition software.

Pointing Devices

While keyboards have been around since the age of typewriters and early computers, mice and other pointing devices are relatively new. Made necessary by the introduction of graphical computer interfaces, these gadgets convert your hand movements into an electronic signal that tells your computer to move a cursor around your screen. This direct and intuitive connection with your computer revolutionized office work — and created a slew of new ergonomic considerations.

Until recently, the mouse was the main pointing device for most office workers. Now we see the increasing use of laptops, tablets, and other portable computers, With the introduction of touchscreens, touchpads, and other alternative pointing options on office computers, we're rapidly moving from the age of "point and click" to an era of "swipe and flick."

Pointing-Device Options

For years, it was safe to assume that most office computers used a mouse as their main pointing device. Not any more. Here's a quick overview of the most common pointing devices that office workers are likely to encounter in the near future.

Mouse

The modern mouse has evolved from a clunky contraption that awkwardly rolled around your mouse pad on a ball (and which gathered a surprising amount of lint) to a sleek, stylish, optically controlled device that glides effortlessly across your desktop and gives you seemingly endless options for clicking and scrolling.

Vertical Mouse

A vertical mouse keeps you from rotating your palm downward to reach your mouse, reducing strain on your wrist and arm. Vertical mice come in two main styles. The first looks like a mouse that has simply been turned on its side. These mice feature slightly different contours to support your hand's sideways position but otherwise operate much like a normal mouse. Other vertical mice look like a joystick that you wrap your fingers around and which you operate with controls on the side and top of the joystick handle.

Trackball

You control a trackball, also known as a roller ball, by rolling a ball with your finger, thumb, or whole hand. It takes up less room on your desktop than a mouse and gives you more cursor control options. For example, if you routinely scroll across a large monitor, a trackball lets you keep rolling continuously across the whole screen without having to lift and reposition it, as you would with a mouse. Trackballs are typically used on a desktop but also come in hand-held models.

Joystick

A true joystick is a lever control that moves in relation to a fixed base while a joystick-style vertical mouse is fixed in position. The most common joystick control that you'll see in the office is the trackpoint, that small eraser-like nub located between the G, H, and B keys on some laptop keyboards. A variety of joystick pointing devices that work much like a vertical mouse are also available.

Touchpad

With a touchpad, you run your fingers over a flat, touch-sensitive surface to move your cursor and execute commands. The touch pad has largely replaced the trackpoint on most laptops now, and touch pads are increasingly common on desktops, as a stand-alone mouse replacement or as a built-in feature on a keyboard.

Touchscreen

Touchscreens were first widely adopted with the introduction of the iPhone in 2007; they came to desktop computers with the introduction of Windows 8 in 2012. This now-familiar interface lets you tap, slide, and swipe directly on your screen. A touchscreen interface may be better suited for mobile devices and other situations in which the screen is horizontal, since reaching out for a vertical screen for long periods can cause arm fatigue.

The Future of Pointing

Clever hackers and innovative product designers are bringing us closer every day to the futuristic, touch-free interface that Tom Cruise operated in the movie "Minority Report." Hackers have already turned Microsoft's Kinect game controller into a pointing device that you can operate by nodding your head and winking. Glove-based mouse replacements have been around for years, used mostly in gaming applications. Manufacturers like Leap Motion have introduced sensor-based pointing interfaces that let you gesture with your fingers to do mouse-like actions without ever touching any hardware. A company called Thalmic Labs is introducing a pointing device in late 2014 that wraps around your forearm and uses electromyography to let you operate your computer by making gestures with your hand. Voice-operated mice can translate your voice commands into cursor movements. A Silicon Valley start-up called Meta is developing a holographic "augmented reality" system that will let you turn any flat surface in your environment into a touchable interface. And it's safe to say that engineers and product designers will keep on figuring out nifty new ways for us to interact with our computers.

Principles-Based Pointing-Device Ergonomics

Given this ongoing proliferation of pointing possibilities, taking a principles-based approach to pointing-device ergonomics makes a lot of sense. The variety of pointing devices available means that it is difficult to anticipate and address all of the details of the ergonomic situation for any one pointing-device. Also, research shows that depending on your job, your age, your gender, other demographic factors, and personal preferences, you may favor one pointing device over another. Finally, as we've seen, new pointing devices are constantly being introduced, and good advice about specific ergonomic practices for these new devices typically lags years behind their introduction. If you're ever in doubt about how to assess your pointing-device ergonomic situation, get back to the basics, the ergonomics principles.

Neutral Posture

You should be able to operate your pointing device with a straight, loose wrist and with your fingers, hand, wrist, and forearm all lined up in a neutral, relaxed position (just as with your keyboard). Your pointing device should be positioned so that your shoulder and upper arm also stay in a neutral position. If your upper arm is positioned awkwardly, you may have to move more at your wrist, a situation you always want to avoid. Instead, you want to position your pointing device so that its movement is initiated from your freely moving elbow.

No Reaching

You never want to have to reach for your pointing device. Reaching even slightly forward or to the side can set off a cascade of postural adaptations that pull your torso and shoulders forward, culminating in the dreaded "mouse shoulder" that I see every day in my massage practice. To avoid this, make sure that your desk surface or keyboard tray is wide enough to accommodate both your keyboard and your pointing device as close together as possible.

If you don't use a numeric keypad in your job, make sure that your keyboard omits the extra 10-key layout. This lets you position your pointing device closer to the midline of both your keyboard and your body, reducing the amount of sideways reaching you have to do.

Proper Height

Your pointing device should be at the same height as your keyboard. Some ergonomic articles advise positioning your mouse or other pointing device above your keyboard, to keep it centered in front of your body. There are two faults in this advice. First, it is hard to find the special gear that lets you position your pointing device like this. Also, positioning it this way requires you to constantly elevate your arm and shoulder.

If you use a keyboard with a built-in touch pad, your pointing device will, of course, already be at the same height as your keyboard.

No Pressure Points

You should be able to gently drape your hand over your pointing device, gripping it so that you can comfortably reach all of the controls. If you use a mouse or similar pointing device, it should fit the contours of your hand. If you use a trackpad, you should be able to reach it without bumping into the edge of your desk or any other obstructions.

No Excessive Motion

If you use a mouse or a vertical mouse, it should glide smoothly and easily over your work surface. Depending on your set-up, you may want to use a cordless model so that you don't have to drag the cord around with the mouse. Your fingers should drape easily over your mouse and be positioned so that you don't have to elevate them or otherwise adopt awkward positions between clicks. If you do a lot of scrolling, consider a mouse with a "fast scroll" button.

Pay Attention to Details

You can adjust both the speed and the sensitivity of most pointing devices using your computer preferences. If your pointing device seems sluggish, overly touchy, or otherwise troublesome, try experimenting with these settings.

Regular breaks

In addition to regular breaks to stand up and leave your desk entirely, give your hands regular breaks from pointing. If you use a mouse, try alternating which hand you use to operate it. You will of course need a mouse design that supports this. On the other hand (sorry), mice are getting so cheap now that even a modest budget could support buying an extra mouse if you use a hand-specific model. Likewise, with the huge variety of alternatives pointing devices available you can use different pointing devices for different tasks. Many graphic designers, for example, switch between a graphics tablet and a mouse depending on whether they are sketching out ideas or laying out a design.

Finally, don't forget about keyboard shortcuts, another great way to take a break from pointing. All operating systems and many individual computer applications let you define keystroke combinations that eliminate the need to use your pointing device for common tasks.

Computer Monitor Ergonomics

Depending on your job, you may spend more time each day looking at your computer monitor than doing almost anything else. The pull of all of that crucial visual information can draw your head forward — and be about as useful as leaning into your car's windshield on a foggy night. Just as when you are driving, you gain no more information by getting your eyes 2 or 3 inches closer to your monitor. You simply contribute to the classic office "turtle posture" — head forward, shoulders slouched, and back rounded. A good ergonomic set-up can encourage a more productive and healthy relationship of your eyes and head with your computer monitor.

Neutral Posture and Proper Height

To promote normal, natural, neutral neck and head posture, your monitor should be positioned with the top edge of the screen display at, or just a little below, eye level, with the monitor tilting away from you just a little so that you look slightly downward as you scan the middle of your screen. This positioning keeps your eyes and the monitor in the same plane and lets you naturally lengthen the back of your neck. Placing your monitor to promote this posture keeps your head, neck, and torso stacked up in a neutral upright position, preventing the constant strain that comes with the forward-head "turtle posture."

No Reaching and No Excessive Motion

Place your monitor directly in front of your body's midline. Placing it even the slightest bit to one side or the other will make you unnecessarily bend and rotate your head, neck, shoulders, and torso, straining muscles and ligaments and impinging nerves and blood vessels. You might not notice any consequences after a day or two or even a week, but I can guarantee you that over time your body will rebel against even such seemingly minor ergonomic indignities.

The optimal distance between your eyes and your monitor depends on the size of your monitor and the range of your peripheral vision. The U.S. Occupational Safety and Health Administration (OSHA) suggests a distance in the range of 20 to 40 inches. Your optimal distance depends on the size of your monitor and its screen resolution. Generally, you'll want to position a big monitor further away and a small monitor closer to you. If you use a very large monitor, then you'll need a very deep desktop or a wall-mounted stand that will let you position it far enough away. In any case, experiment with your monitor placement to find a distance that lets you easily see your screen without any peering or straining.

By the way, I have seen many articles and blog posts that recommend placing your monitor at arms length. This may work for a narrow range of monitor sizes, but it is not a trustworthy rule of thumb.

If you find yourself straining to see your screen even after you have done all that you can to optimize your monitor's position, remember, that you can also adjust the font size in most computer applications. I work mostly on a 13-inch laptop, and using this trick has helped me prevent neck and eye strain as while writing this book.

If you use multiple computer monitors, make sure that your workstation lets you position yourself directly in front of each of them as you change your focus. If you use both monitors equally, make sure that you can easily turn your whole body and keyboard toward the one you are working on. If you have a primary monitor and an auxiliary one, place the main one right in front of you and the extra one off to the side.

Pay Attention to Details

Regardless of whether you are standing, perching, sitting, or kneeling, the relationship between your computer monitor and your eyes, head, and neck remains pretty much the same. So, if you use an adjustable-height desk, or if you change to and from different height workstations during the day, make sure that the relationships between your monitor and keyboard and mouse remain consistent. This can be harder than you might think, because some sit-stand workstations adjust each component separately.

If you use a document holder, the ideal place to put it is directly in front of you between your keyboard and monitor. If that isn't possible with your set-up, place the monitor holder next to your monitor as close to it as possible.

If you use bifocals, you are at high risk for "turtle posture." The classic head-up-eyes-looking-down posture that comes with bifocal use is a recipe for neck pain and back strain. Instead of straining, lower your monitor and/or tilt the screen up toward you. If you spend long stretches at your computer, you could find it well worth the investment to get single-vision lenses at a focal length designed for your computer work.

Regular breaks

Staring into a computer monitor for hours on end can be rough on your eyes, causing fatigue and dryness. Some have labeled this condition "computer vision syndrome." Whatever you call it, you can prevent it by taking regular breaks. Optometrists recommend the "20/20/20" break: Every twenty minutes take a break to look at something twenty feet away for twenty seconds.

Environment

Lighting is the main environmental hazard that can interfere with you monitor ergonomics. Don't let glare from windows and overhead lights disrupt your ability to see what's on your screen. Ideally, you want to position the surface of your monitor perpendicular to any light sources. If you sit by a window, position your desk at a right angle to it. If you have bright overhead lighting, position your monitor at a right angle to it. If you can't control your lighting and/or monitor position, then you may need to get an anti-glare filter. You can also adjust the brightness and contrast on your monitor, of course. Finally, keep your monitor screen clean. A blurry, dusty screen is a surefire recipe for more peering.

Laptop Ergonomics

Laptop computers have outsold desktops for years now and have become the primary computer for legions of office workers.

The main ergonomic challenge with a laptop is the fixed relationship between the keyboard and monitor. If your hands are positioned correctly, then you have to crane your neck to see the screen. If you position the screen as you would a desktop monitor, then you have to awkwardly reach upward to use the keyboard.

There are three ergonomic strategies to help you cope with this situation.

Strategy 1: Use Your Laptop Like a Desktop

If you primarily use your laptop at your desk for long stretches, think of it as the CPU tower that came with your old desktop computer. Then attach a monitor, keyboard, and pointing device just as you would to your traditional desktop. There are a number of ways to accomplish this.

If you need to attach a printer or other peripheral devices to your computer, connect to a local network, or use multiple monitors, you'll probably need a commercial docking station. Those stations typically include a power source, network connections, and extra USB and other device ports. Some models include hardware that accommodates multiple monitors; some include locks and other security measures. You can choose from models specifically designed for a particular line of laptops and "universal" models that can work with any laptop.

If your computing needs are more basic, you can simply attach an external monitor, keyboard, and pointing device directly to your laptop without a docking station.

If space is limited or your budget is tight, you can create a desktop set-up that works for you. Keyboards and pointing devices are cheaper than monitors, so the most economical solution is to elevate your laptop screen using a commercial laptop stand or a homemade platform. Then attach an external keyboard and mouse. This essentially turns your laptop into a monitor. If you often work remotely, you can use this kind of set-up at home or even on the road. Just pack a keyboard and mouse in your bag and improvise a laptop stand in your hotel room using books, boxes, or other items at hand.

If your work requires a large monitor but you have no room for external input devices, you can simply attach a large monitor to your laptop and use its built-in keyboard and pointing device.

You get the idea. By thinking of your laptop as a CPU tower, you can use it just as you would a desktop computer.

All too often, though, you are probably stuck with work to do and just you and your laptop (and, hopefully, a standing-height counter to work on). The next two strategies help in this situation.

Strategy 2: Favor a Typing Position

When it's just you and your laptop in a conference room, a motel room, or a coffee shop, you have to compromise ergonomically. The fixed relationship between your screen and keyboard means that either your wrists or your neck will be challenged as you use your laptop. You'll have to position your keyboard to save your wrists or your screen to save your neck.

Because your neck muscles are stronger than your wrist muscles, it's generally better to position your laptop to favor typing. So apply the same principles to your portable laptop set-up that you would for a keyboard set-up.

Of course this means that you'll have to look down at your laptop screen. Depending on your height and other body dimensions, this can be either really uncomfortable or a quite manageable situation. As I wrote this book, having my laptop set up with the keyboard positioned to favor my wrists and arms worked just fine. But that's just me and my anatomy (and an unusual amount of office fitness self-care knowledge). Depending on the unique relationship between your arms, shoulders, neck, and head, you may have to bring some postural awareness to bear to keep your neck and back safe and comfortable (more on this in the next chapter on posture).

I work standing up, which makes it harder to slouch. When you sit to use a laptop, most people have a strong tendency to slouch and to peer into the laptop screen. That leads to the dreaded rounded-back "turtle posture." Since you have consciously and deliberately set up your laptop to favor using your keyboard, this is not a surprise. To reverse this slouch, bring your awareness to bear and pull your torso, neck, and head into an upright, neutral posture as you type (again, more on this in the posture chapter).

Strategy 3: Favor a Viewing Position

When using your laptop primarily to read or otherwise look at information, set it up to favor a viewing position, positioning your laptop screen as you would a desktop monitor. So you want to apply the same principles to your portable laptop set-up that you would to a monitor set-up.

The viewing position will, of course, compromise your ability to reach and use your laptop's keyboard and pointing device. If you aren't doing too much keying and pointing, you can cope with this by simply reaching for the keys and touch pad as best you can.

If you are primarily looking at the screen but also using the keyboard a fair amount, it can be useful to try to better align your forearms to the plane of your keyboard. If you have angled your keyboard upward to place your screen higher, you might lower your sitting surface a bit to drop your elbows lower, putting your forearms in roughly the same plane as the laptop keyboard. This will, of course, also alter your head's position in relation to the monitor, so it is important to consider each of the variables — screen height, keyboard angle, and forearm angle — and experiment to find a reasonable compromise position.

I have, of course, played with this idea a lot. I occasionally take a break from standing to kneel in a Balans-style chair. When I do, I put my laptop on a three-ring binder (tall side away from me) to elevate the screen, which angles the keyboard upward (if you try this hack, be sure to choose a three-ring-binder that has a textured surface so that your laptop doesn't slide around). I then drop the chair height down so that my forearms angle upward at about the same angle as the keyboard. It's still an imperfect set-up, but by compromising just a bit on monitor height, keyboard angle, and forearm angle I can both look at the screen and do a little typing comfortably. I also discovered that I could achieve the same compromise when standing up by slightly raising the surface of my standing desk and going through the same adjustments. In either case, when I go back to primarily writing, I adjust my set-up to favor the keyboard.

Tablet and Smart Phone Ergonomics

Laptop computer ergonomics are troublesome enough. Tablets, smart phones, and other tiny, portable-computing gadgets take ergonomic challenges to new heights.

As you may have noticed, we are buying these gizmos like crazy. Tablet PC sales are projected to outnumber desktop and laptop PC sales combined by 2015. And just think about how quickly we have all switched from old flip phones to smart phones in the past five years. Many of these are truly personal computing devices, used mainly at home and at school, but more and more of our professional work is being done on them, too.

Almost all of these devices now have a touch-screen interface. The intuitive nature of this integration of viewing surface and data-entry surface explains their appeal, but it also creates some problematic ergonomic scenarios, leading to new ways to get eyestrain, headaches, back pain, shoulder pain, and wrist pain.

Because they are so new, there is little research or ergonomic conventional wisdom to guide the use of tablets and smart phones. As Anna Pereira and her colleagues at UC-Berkeley noted in 2013, "Only a handful of studies have evaluated the musculoskeletal risks associated with mobile devices."

So our best bet is to fall back on the ergonomic principles set out earlier in this chapter.

Neutral Posture, No Reaching, and Proper Height

As with a laptop, the viewing screen and the input device are fixed in relationship to one another. As you both peer into the screen and swipe your fingers across it, the tendency is to curl up into a rounded-back, hunched-over position — not exactly a neutral posture. As with any computer set-up, you need to position your portable gadgets so that you can keep your spine vertical, your neck un-flexed, and your shoulders, arms, and hands in as natural a position as possible.

Just as with a laptop computer, you can apply three strategies to achieve this.

Strategy 1: Use Your Tablet Like a Desktop

Depending on which tablet model you have, you may be able to buy or make a docking station so that you can use your tablet like a desktop computer. Commercial docking stations that include a monitor, keyboard, and mouse are available for Windows tablets, and it's not too hard to put together components to make your own Android-tablet docking station. There is no official support for an external mouse or monitor for the iPad, but external keyboards are widely available, and it's easy to find instructions online to jailbreak your iPad and use apps that let you add an external monitor and navigate your iPad screen with a Bluetooth mouse.

Strategy 2: Favor a Typing or Drawing Position

If you use your tablet or smart phone primarily to enter information, your best bet is to use an external keyboard. Wireless, external keyboards are available for virtually all tablets and smart phones. Since they are wireless, you can fairly easily position the keyboard optimally as described earlier and also position your screen so that you don't have to flex your neck to view it. If you use your device's touch-screen keyboard, position the screen so that your hands can easily reach it with your arms and shoulders in a neutral position while craning your neck as little possible to glance at the screen to verify your input.

If you use your tablet or smart phone to draw or manipulate images, consider using a stylus, which, of course, results in a position very much like working with pencil and paper. Many artists, illustrators, and designers favor a stylus over a finger input, and there is some evidence (e.g., Badam et al. 2014) that styli are more accurate. Regardless of whether you are working with your finger or a stylus, position your tablet or phone so that you can reach it comfortably, with your wrists in neutral and your upper arms hanging comfortably at your side. You'll inevitably crane your neck forward a bit as you work, of course, but by experimenting with the angle and position of the screen you can arrive at an intermediate position that let's you work with your images without craning your neck too much, just as you did back at your old-fashioned paper-and-pencil drawing table.

Strategy 3: Favor a Viewing Position

If you use your tablet or smart phone primarily to view information on the screen, position your device much as you would an external computer monitor.

Most commercial tablets include or offer as an option a stand that lets you position your screen in a near-vertical position. Ideally, you'll want to place the stand on a surface that is about even with your eye height. If there's not an appropriate-height table or cabinet handy, you can raise the stand using a box or something similar. You'll have to reach out to navigate from page to page, of course, but the light stress of occasional reaching for the screen is a small price to pay for a properly positioned neck and head. If you don't have a commercial tablet stand available, you can improvise one with a three-ring-binder, rolled-up jacket, backpack, pillow, couch cushion, etc.

Some tablets are now as small as smart phones, and some smart phones are as big as small tablets. Still, most smart-phone screens are generally too small to use for viewing from a stand, so you'll have to hold them in your hand. Many people end up holding their smart phones around stomach level and flexing their necks to peer down into the screen. A better position for viewing your smart-phone screen is to tuck your elbows in at your side and angle your forearms up as high as you comfortably can. This positions the screen closer to your eyes and by tucking your elbows in you reduce the stress on your arms and shoulders of holding up your smart phone. You still have to look down a bit to see the screen, but this position requires much less neck flexion than holding the phone in your lap.

Minimize Fatigue and Static Load

It's possible to hold a tablet or smart phone with both hands and to operate it with your thumbs, but this creates undue strain, as early smart-phone adopters discovered when they came down with a case of "Blackberry thumb." Holding your phone or tablet in one hand with as neutral a grip as possible and operating it with the other hand is a better choice.

Interestingly, Taebeum Ryu and two fellow South Korean engineers (2013) reported that users showed little preference for their dominant hand when operating a smart phone — and little difference in performance between their dominant and non-dominant hands. You may have already discovered that yourself.

No Excessive Motion

No matter how neutral your posture and how smooth your data entry motions, imperfect tablet and smart-phone interfaces can make your fingers, hands, and wrists work harder than is ideal. Using voice commands, like the Siri feature on an iPhone, and apps that reduce the number of keystrokes required to complete common tasks can minimize this problem.

When making phone calls, using a headset or speakerphone keeps you from having to hold the phone up or, heaven forbid, cradling it between your ear and shoulder.

When drawing or doing other detailed work on the screen, using a stylus offers more accuracy and precision than a finger with less extra motion (and less frustration).

Finally, when using a smart phone or tablet, try to keep messages short and use abbreviations. This is already a common and expected convention with portable computing, but it bears keeping in mind (especially for long-winded old-timers like me).

Pay Attention to Details

Small screens can be rough on your eyes. Your first line of defense here is to get as large a screen as possible. You can also adjust the contrast and brightness of your screen via operating system settings. Many tablet and smart-phone apps let you increase the type size, further reducing eye strain.

Of course, choosing a larger screen may mean that your tablet or phone is a bit heavier. Lighter is better with portable computing — most of the time. Keep this trade-off in mind as you pick out your tablet or smart phone.

Finally, you always want to keep a firm grip a device that costs several hundred dollars. Investing in a case with a nonslip texture will make it easier to hold on to and less likely to drop your tablet or phone.

Telephone Ergonomics

Phones have been around a lot longer than computers, and you will still see one on almost every office desk. Because they're so well-entrenched and because they do only one thing, telephone ergonomics are pretty straightforward.

Neutral Posture

The most common ergonomic problem with telephone use is the temptation to cradle the phone between your shoulder and ear. That original hands-free method of using the phone ranks right after prolonged sitting as a candidate for the most body-wrecking thing you can do in an office. Telephone headsets are so ubiquitous and affordable nowadays that there is really no excuse for engaging in this barbaric, neck-wrenching practice. A good headset costs barely 20 bucks, and you can buy even fancy wireless headsets for well under $100. Any of these headsets will free up your hands so you can take notes and look up information as you talk on the phone.

If for some reason you can't use a headset, a padded cushion for the back of your phone handset can mitigate the posture-altering effects of cradling the phone. If you work in a private office or have unusually tolerant co-workers, a speakerphone is another hands-free phone option.

No Reaching

The best place to put your phone is as close to the edge of your desk on your nondominant-hand side. This keeps your dominant hand free for note-taking and other chores. Keeping the phone as close to you as possible also reduces the need to lean forward, which can put strain on your back, especially if get lots of calls and frequently reach for your phone.

Minimize Fatigue and Static Load

Dragging a cord along with your telephone handset and then holding it up and out of the way as you talk can strain your arms and shoulders. A light, cordless handset can minimize the effort of holding your phone for prolonged calls.

Developing Better Ergonomics Habits

Add a Tiny Habit

Recall B.J. Fogg's recipe for a Tiny Habit: After I [existing habit/anchor], I will [new tiny behavior]. Some ideas for improving your ergonomic habits:

- After I sit down, I will adjust my chair height so that my hips are a little higher than my knees.
- After I adjust my sit-stand desk to a different position, I will make sure the height lets my arms hang freely and my wrists and hands stay comfortably in a neutral position as I work.
- After I arrive at my standing desk, I will position my footrest so that I can easily reach it.
- After I start up the treadmill at my walking workstation, I will take one or two long strides to make sure that I won't kick the motor casing as I walk.
- After I turn on my computer, I will align my belly button with the "B" key on my keyboard.
- After I turn on my monitor, I will wipe the screen to remove any dust and adjust the contrast and brightness.
- After I check my email, I will take a 20/20 vision break (look at something 20 feet away for 20 seconds).
- After I open my laptop, I will adjust the keyboard to position my hands and wrists in neutral (when favoring typing).
- After I open my laptop, I will position the screen (when favoring viewing).
- After I find an article to read online, I will increase the font size with my browser controls.
- After I answer my smart phone, I will attach a headset (or switch to speaker mode) if it looks like it's going to be a long call.

Modify a Habit Loop

Recall Charles Duhigg's habit loop and how you can manipulate each part of it — the cue, the routine, and the reward — as well as the underlying craving. When it comes to ergonomic habits, it is usually your equipment that drives the habit loop, so most of these habit loop modifications involve adjusting or changing your gear. Some ideas:

- Slouching is a classic habit among the chair-bound. Sometimes it's enough to just become aware of your posture to realize that you are slouching; sometimes pain in your middle and low back alerts you. You are typically cued to slouch by your ergonomic set-up — for example, a chair that doesn't support a neutral posture. The ensuing routine is for you to slump forward to accommodate your gear. Your reward is a feeling of apparent relaxation. The quickest way to break this habit loop is to get a chair with lumbar support or to add a lumbar roll to your existing chair. The gentle nudge of the lumbar support will cue you to keep a normal slightly forward curve in your low back, which makes it all but impossible for you to slouch.

- Another classic office habit is craning your neck to peer into a poorly situated monitor. You can prevent or redress this "turtle posture" by hacking the habit loop that puts you there. The cue is the draw of the information on your computer screen. Just as you peer forward into your car windshield on a foggy night, knowing full well that putting your head two inches forward won't actually help you avoid any obstacles that suddenly appear, your routine is to draw your head forward in the hope that you might better see a document or spreadsheet. To disrupt this loop, experiment with enlarging the fonts in the applications you routinely use, adjusting the brightness and contrast of your display, and/or repositioning the monitor.

- Most of us, when we get a new computer, simply accept the standard-issue flat keyboard and track pad or mouse that come with it. This is more of a ritual than a habit, of course, but it still gets us in the routine of turning our palms downward as we work, which is a decidedly un-neutral ergonomic position. Ordering a split-tray ergonomic keyboard and/or a vertical mouse with your new computer can break this habit loop.

- Plenty of office workers get in the habit of maintaining a cluttered desktop. The cue: something physical arrives — a piece of paper, a new gadget, some swag from your last conference. The routine: just toss it in the pile. The reward: you don't have to deal with the implications of your new acquisition (and you look busy). A problem with this habit is that eventually items that you regularly need or want to use disappear into the pile or are pushed out of reach. One solution is to dedicate an area for clutter and another for stuff you actually use. A better solution is to adopt a productivity system like David Allen's "Getting Things Done," and deal with new materials as they arrive.

Adopt a Practice

Try one or more of the following established practices that naturally include ergonomic awareness. These practices always include training in how to position yourself in relation to your equipment so as to improve performance and avoid injury. Even though your coach or teacher may not articulate that in ergonomic terms, the goals are very similar to the ergonomic ideal of balancing productivity and comfort. Few of the practices mentioned are directly transferable to office work, but they can get you in the habit of working comfortably with your gear.

- Learn touch typing. This, of course, applies directly to most office jobs. If you are still a hunt-and-peck typist, learning to touch-type can reduce the strain on your wrists and hands and neck caused by peering down at your hands.
- Take up a sport that involves gear or apparatus. Sports like baseball, river rafting, rowing, and many others require you to master both your own movement and the control of some equipment. An added benefit is the contribution to your overall fitness.
- Learn a musical instrument. Most musical instruction either explicitly or implicitly includes education in ergonomic principles like maintaining a neutral posture, not reaching, minimizing fatigue, and moving efficiently.
- Master a craft or trade like spinning yarn, weaving cloth on a loom, woodworking, masonry, or pottery. Not only will you have some cool new artifacts decorating your home and

office. You will also have mastered another set of skills that embody good ergonomic practice.

Take a Plunge

Go nuts! Throw a monkey wrench into your current set-up to create instant, widespread change. Some ideas:

- Change jobs to find a more ergonomically savvy employer. The Seattle software company Tableau made headlines in 2014 when they bought adjustable sit-stand desks for all 1,200 of their employees. Look for an outfit like that in your field and city.
- If you can't get the ergonomic set-up you need at work, strike out on your own. Self-employment, of course, gives you complete control over your ergonomic set-up. (But bear in mind this wisdom I once heard: "You can work for yourself and have the illusion of independence, or you can work for a big company and have the illusion of security. Either way, it's an illusion.")
- Get a sit-stand desk, a standing desk, or a treadmill desk. Many of the classic ergonomic challenges of office work result from being in a sitting position all day. Changing the foundation of your ergonomic set-up by getting up and moving can set into motion many other ergonomic benefits.
- Become an ergonomics consultant. In the U.S., the Board of Certification in Professional Ergonomics (BCPE) certifies ergonomics professionals.

Suggested Reading

The Chair, Galen Cranz

Sources

"Human Factors and Ergonomics." Wikipedia, the Free Encyclopedia, August 1, 2013. http://en.wikipedia.org/

"OSHA Ergonomic Solutions: Computer Workstations eTool." U.S. Department Deparment of Labor Occupational Safety & Health Administration. https://www.osha.gov/

"Safety and Health Topics: Ergonomics." U.S. Department of Labor Occupational Safety & Health Administration. https://www.osha.gov/

Amick, Benjamin C. III, Michelle M. PhD Robertson CPE, Kelly DeRango, Lianna Bazzani, Anne Moore, Ted Rooney, and Ron Harrist. "Effect of Office Ergonomics Intervention on Reducing Musculoskeletal Symptoms." Spine December 15, 2003 28, no. 24 (2003): 2706–11.

Hendrick, Hal W. "Good Ergonomics Is Good Economics." In Good Ergonomics Is Good Economics. Human Factors and Ergonomics Society, 1996.

MacLeod, Dan. "10 Principles of Ergonomics." Dan MacLeod: Ergonomics Consultant. http://www.danmacleod.com/ErgoForYou/10_principles_of_ergonomics.htm.

Chairs and Desks

Cranz, Galen. The Chair: Rethinking Culture, Body, and Design. New edition edition. New York: W. W. Norton & Company, 2013.

Gerr, F, M Marcus, D Ortiz, B White, W Jones, S Cohen, E Gentry, A Edwards, and E Bauer. "Computer Users' Postures and Associations with Workstation Characteristics." AIHAJ: A Journal for the Science of Occupational and Environmental Health and Safety 61, no. 2 (April 2000): 223–30.

Horton, Stuart J., Gillian M. Johnson, and Margot A. Skinner. "Changes in Head and Neck Posture Using an Office Chair with and without Lumbar Roll Support." Spine 35, no. 12 (2010): E542–E548.

John, Dinesh, David Bassett, Dixie Thompson, Jeffrey Fairbrother, and Debora Baldwin. "Effect of Using a Treadmill Workstation on Performance of Simulated Office Work Tasks." Journal of Physical Activity & Health 6, no. 5 (September 2009): 617–24.

Mueller, Guenter F., and Marc Hassenzahl. "Sitting Comfort of Ergonomic Office Chairs–Developed Versus Intuitive Evaluation." International Journal of Occupational Safety and Ergonomics 16, no. 3 (2010): 369–74.

Robertson, Michelle, Benjamin C. Amick III, Kelly DeRango, Ted Rooney, Lianna Bazzani, Ron Harrist, and Anne Moore. "The Effects of an Office Ergonomics Training and Chair Intervention on Worker Knowledge, Behavior and Musculoskeletal Risk." Applied Ergonomics 40, no. 1 (January 2009): 124–35.

Straker, Leon, Rebecca A. Abbott, Marina Heiden, Svend Erik Mathiassen, and Allan Toomingas. "Sit–stand Desks in Call Centres: Associations of Use and Ergonomics Awareness with Sedentary Behavior." Applied Ergonomics 44, no. 4 (July 2013): 517–22.

Keyboard, Mouse, and Pointing Devices

"USB Typewriter." http://www.usbtypewriter.com/

Baker, Nancy A., Norman P. Gustafson, and Joan Rogers. "The Association Between Rheumatoid Arthritis Related Structural Changes in Hands and Computer Keyboard Operation." Journal of Occupational Rehabilitation 20, no. 1 (March 1, 2010): 59–68.

Barrero, Aurora, David Melendi, Xabiel G. Pañeda, Roberto García, and Sergio Cabrero. "An Empirical Investigation Into Text Input Methods for Interactive Digital Television Applications." International Journal of Human-Computer Interaction 30, no. 4 (2014): 321–41.

Cook, Catherine, Robin Burgess-Limerick, and Shona Papalia. "The Effect of Upper Extremity Support on Upper Extremity Posture and Muscle Activity during Keyboard Use." Applied Ergonomics, The Occlusion Technique, 35, no. 3 (May 2004): 285–92.

Hedge, Alan, Singe Morimoto, and Daniel Mccrobie. "Effects of Keyboard Tray Geometry on Upper Body Posture and Comfort." Ergonomics 42, no. 10 (October 1999): 1333–49.

Iwakiri, Kazuyuki, Ippei Mori, Midori Sotoyama, Kaori Horiguchi, Takanori Ochiai, Hiroshi Jonai, and Susumu Saito. "Survey on Visual and Musculoskeletal Symptoms in VDT Workers." Sangyo Eiseigaku Zasshi 46, no. 6 (2004): 201–12.

Kotani, K., L. H. Barrero, D. L. Lee, and J. T. Dennerlein. "Effect of Horizontal Position of the Computer Keyboard on Upper Extremity Posture and Muscular Load during Computer Work." Ergonomics 50, no. 9 (2007): 1419–32.

Lee, Tzu-Hsien. "Ergonomic Comparison of Operating a Built-in Touch-Pad Pointing Device and a Trackball Mouse on Posture and Muscle Activity." Perceptual and Motor Skills 101, no. 3 (December 2005): 730–36.

Marklin, Richard W., and Guy G. Simoneau. "Design Features of Alternative Computer Keyboards: A Review of Experimental Data." Journal of Orthopaedic & Sports Physical Therapy 34, no. 10 (October 1, 2004): 638–49.

McLoone, Hugh E., Melissa Jacobson, Chau Hegg, and Peter W. Johnson. "User-Centered Design and Evaluation of a next Generation Fixed-Split Ergonomic Keyboard." Work: A Journal of Prevention, Assessment and Rehabilitation 37, no. 4 (2010): 445–56.

Pascarelli, E F, and J J Kella. "Soft-Tissue Injuries Related to Use of the Computer Keyboard. A Clinical Study of 53 Severely Injured Persons." Journal of Occupational Medicine.: Official Publication of the Industrial Medical Association 35, no. 5 (May 1993): 522–32.

Pogue, David. "Why Touch Screens Will Not Take Over." Scientific American, December 18, 2012. http://www.scientificamerican.com/

Smith, M J, B T Karsh, F T Conway, W J Cohen, C A James, J J Morgan, K Sanders, and D J Zehel. "Effects of a Split Keyboard Design and Wrist Rest on Performance, Posture, and Comfort." Human Factors 40, no. 2 (June 1998): 324–36.

Willey, Marc S. "The Effects of User Friendly Keyboard Slope Modifications on Wrist Postures When Keyboarding." Work: A Journal of Prevention, Assessment and Rehabilitation 39, no. 4 (2011): 441–44.

Monitors

Iwakiri, Kazuyuki, Ippei Mori, Midori Sotoyama, Kaori Horiguchi, Takanori Ochiai, Hiroshi Jonai, and Susumu Saito. "Survey on Visual and Musculoskeletal Symptoms in VDT Workers." Sangyo Eiseigaku Zasshi 46, no. 6 (2004): 201–12.

Johnston, Venerina, Nerina L. Jimmieson, Gwendolen Jull, and Tina Souvlis. "Quantitative Sensory Measures Distinguish Office Workers with Varying Levels of Neck Pain and Disability." Pain 137, no. 2 (July 15, 2008): 257–65.

Kothiyal, Kamal, and Ane Marte Bjørnerem. "Effects of Computer Monitor Setting on Muscular Activity, User Comfort and Acceptability in Office Work." Work: A Journal of Prevention, Assessment and Rehabilitation 32, no. 2 (January 1, 2009): 155–63.

Laptops, Tablets, and Smart Phones

American Occupational Therapy Association. "Preventing Pain: Using Smart Phones Wisely." States News Service, December 13, 2011.

Armbrüster, C., C. Sutter, and M. Ziefle. "Notebook Input Devices Put to the Age Test: The Usability of Trackpoint and Touchpad for Middle-Aged Adults." Ergonomics 50, no. 3 (2007): 426–45.

Kaufman, David Micah. "Tech Ergonomics: Laptops, Tablets, and Smartphones." Safety Daily Advisor — BLR, September 17, 2012. http://safetydailyadvisor.blr.com/

Kelaher, Dan, Todd Nay, Brad Lawrence, Sabrina Lamar, and Carolyn M Sommerich. "An Investigation of the Effects of Touchpad Location within a Notebook Computer." Applied Ergonomics 32, no. 1 (February 2001): 101–10.

Lai, Chih-Chun, and Chih-Fu Wu. "Size Effects on the Touchpad, Touchscreen, and Keyboard Tasks of Netbooks." Perceptual and Motor Skills 115, no. 2 (October 2012): 481–501.

Pereira, Anna, Tevis Miller, Yi-Min Huang, Dan Odell, and David Rempel. "Holding a Tablet Computer with One Hand: Effect of Tablet Design Features on Biomechanics and Subjective Usability among Users with Small Hands." Ergonomics 56, no. 9 (September 2013): 1363–75.

Ryu, Taebeum, Jihyoun Lim, Joobong Song, Myung Hwan Yun, and Moonsoo Shin. "Performance Comparison between the Preferred Right and Preferred Left Hands in Text Entry Using Qwerty Touch Keyboard Smartphones." International Journal of Industrial Ergonomics 43, no. 5 (September 2013): 400–405.

Sommerich, C. M., R. Ward, K. Sikdar, J. Payne, and L. Herman. "A Survey of High School Students with Ubiquitous Access to Tablet PCs." Ergonomics 50, no. 5 (2007): 706–27.

Young, Justin G., Matthieu Trudeau, Dan Odell, Kim Marinelli, and Jack T. Dennerlein. "Touch-Screen Tablet User Configurations and Case-Supported Tilt Affect Head and Neck Flexion Angles." Work: A Journal of Prevention, Assessment and Rehabilitation 41, no. 1 (2012): 81–91.

This is a partial list of sources consulted as I wrote this chapter, including only items mentioned or referred to above. For a full list of everything I read as I prepared this chapter, please visit sitless.com/chapter4

Chapter 5
Posture in the Office

Good posture can keep you out of a lot of trouble, and bad posture can get you into it. Your posture habits can determine the difference between a lifetime of chronic pain and injury and one of grace and ease.

Ergonomics is about your relationship with your furniture and devices. Posture is about your relationship with your body. You've been in that relationship your whole life, from your mother's womb right up to this moment. It is no surprise, then, that posture is one of your most deeply ingrained habitual behaviors. In fact, some aspects of posture go even deeper than habit — just as hardwired as your breath and heartbeat. The shape of your bones, the unconscious engagement of deep muscles that hold you upright, the automatic position corrections that your vestibular and vision systems make, the reflexive responses of your nervous system that keep you upright and balanced all affect your posture but lie beyond your conscious control.

You have a great deal of control over other aspects of posture. You can change your muscle tone and the flexibility of your joints with movement and exercise, as described in the final chapter. You can control your weight with diet and exercise. You can choose the clothing and shoes that you wear. You can learn to monitor and consciously change the way you position of yourself in space with the body awareness practices shown in this chapter. All of which can encourage you to cultivate new habits that improve your posture.

Why Posture Matters

When your body is positioned properly, your breath comes more easily, your digestive system works better, and other systems in your body work as they're supposed to. As you slump or slouch, cross your legs, or otherwise reposition your limbs, head, and torso into unnatural postures, here's what happens:

- Your muscles, tendons, and ligaments are stretched out or scrunched up, putting undue stress on your joints and spine and altering your ability to freely and comfortably move. All of this makes you more vulnerable to sprains, strains, and similar injuries.
- Your lungs' ability to expand is constrained by your slumping rib cage, which impairs your ability to breath deeply and naturally.
- Your blood and lymph vessels are constricted, impeding your circulatory system.
- Your nerves are impinged, causing tingling and numbness and disrupting the normal flow of nerve impulses between your central nervous system and the rest of your body.
- Your stomach, intestines, liver, and other internal organs are displaced and distorted, interfering with your ability to optimally digest your food and process bodily wastes.
- Your psychological well-being can be diminished, your mood reflecting the defeated posture of your body. This can even lead to your being thought of more negatively by others who see you in this state.

Sometimes you can feel the effects of bad posture right away — headaches, back pain, a "dead" feeling in your arms and hands, fatigue. Other effects of poor posture can take years to manifest. Like the frog placed in a pot of water who doesn't notice that it is slowly boiling, you may not be aware of the consequences of poor posture until it's too late.

So how do you recognize and prevent poor posture? More to the point, how can you develop good posture habits? Most of this chapter focuses on that, but first let's look more closely at how your mood affects your posture and your posture affects your mood.

The Psychology of Posture

Your posture both reflects and determines how you feel. If you feel happy, you smile. But you'll also feel happy if you're forced to smile by holding a pencil between your teeth (Strack et al 1988).

When your shoulders are back, your torso erect, and your gaze level, you feel like a million bucks — like a powerful silverback gorilla among a bunch of nattering chimpanzees. If your shoulders are slumped and your head is drooping, you're more likely to feel like a melancholic sheep being pushed around by a collie.

In classic office posture your head drops forward into a hangdog look, shoulders rolled inward and forward with your back bowed from slouching, mimicking the symptoms of depression. You may not have been depressed when you started your office job, but after a few years of modeling dispirited behavior with your office worker slouch you may understandably begin to feel a little down (after Briñol et al 2009).

On the other hand, if you cultivate an alert, engaged, powerful posture at work you'll feel better and even be perceived more favorably. Fascinating research by business school professors Dana Carney and Amy Cuddy reveals that simply adopting a powerful pose for just one minute makes you feel more powerful. They found that the body actually changes when placed in positions traditionally seen as dominant and powerful, such as putting your hands on your hips or sitting back in your chair with your feet on your desk. Testosterone levels increase and cortisol levels decrease in blood samples drawn after just 60 seconds of this kind of power posing.

Cuddy elaborated on this finding in a subsequent experiment and discovered that interview candidates who briefly adopted a power pose before — but not during — a job interview were more likely to be offered the position. The poise, confidence, and enthusiasm conferred by the power pose adopted before the interview carried over into the interview itself after just one minute of power-pose preparation (Cuddy 2102).

Your posture may even be more powerful than the position you hold at work. Li Huang and her business-school colleagues revisited earlier research on the relationship between posture and assigned hierarchical roles (2011). A series of experiments that tested the way people thought and acted in contrived situations showed that

107

"posture mattered more than role in determining thought and behavior." So, theoretically anyway, you can promote yourself to a powerful, decision-making position at work simply by adopting more powerful postures.

This reminds me of what one of my massage school teachers once said. "Give ulcers; don't get 'em." If all you have to do to be perceived as more powerful and authoritative is to assume power postures, then why not use those findings to gain power at work and advance your career. I would never advocate abusing this power, but if it gives you a leg up in office politics, then so be it.

Recognizing Good Posture

It's easy enough to spot bad posture. A glance around your office will almost certainly spot a couple of co-workers slumped forward or sliding out of their chairs or sitting on a foot, crossing their legs, or otherwise contorting their bodies as they try to find comfortable work positions. Look at people in any public setting and you'll see the postural accumulation of such habits — heads jutting out in front of torsos, shoulders slumped, backs rounded, arms hanging with the palm of the hand facing backwards, bellies jutting out over forwardly tilted pelvises. If your reaction is like mine, it will almost hurt just to look at such postures.

Then look at people in other contexts: athletes on a playing field mingling before a game, dancers poised to go on stage, movie stars on a red carpet, a public speaker at a lectern, your personal trainer at the gym, hunter-gatherers in a TV documentary. There, you see the results of better posture habits: heads poised elegantly atop long, relaxed necks; squared up shoulders draping over upright torsos, arms swinging freely; tucked-in stomachs over aligned lower bodies. You can almost feel their confidence and grace, and you want to embody it in yourself.

Most of us, of course, fall somewhere between those extremes. Your body is astonishingly forgiving and resilient, so even if you've had a desk job for years, you may not — yet — exhibit the bad posture traits described above. Even if you're an ambitious and physically active desk worker, the positions you adopt at work all day may keep you from achieving the perfect posture of an Olympic athlete or a professional dancer.

Observation:
The Yogi Berra Approach to Posture

Baseball legend Yogi Berra once said, "You can observe a lot just by watching." As with many of Yogi's observations, once you get past the unintentional humor and grammatical awkwardness, you encounter some profound insight.

You can learn a lot about your posture just by looking at it. Stand in front of a full-length mirror (in your underwear at home; in appropriate attire at work) with your feet a little less than shoulder-width apart. Close your eyes. Shake your arms out. Wiggle your torso a bit. And then settle into what feels like a neutral posture, open your eyes, and take a look at yourself. As you scan your posture in the mirror, don't make any judgements about what you see or make any hypotheses about what your observations might mean. Just watch for now.

First look at yourself head-on.

- Is your head level with your eyes and ears directly opposite one another?
- Is your head centered over your neck and torso, or is it shifted to one side?
- Does your neck rise straight up out of your torso, or is it offset or tilting to one side?
- Are your shoulders level, or is one higher than the other?
- Is your torso centered over your lower body?
- Are your hips at the same level, or is one higher than the other?
- Are your knees oriented, with both pointing the same direction with a similar alignment of the kneecaps?
- Do your feet naturally point straight ahead, a little inward, a little outward?

Ideally, you want to appear symmetrical from side to side, but practically no one has achieved this, so don't worry at all if you look a little lopsided.

Now, turn sideways to the mirror and position a second mirror so that you can look at yourself from the side without turning your head.

109

- Is your head centered over your torso with your ears directly over your shoulders? Is it forward of the midline of your torso?
- Is your head level, your jaw line parallel to the floor, or is your head cocked a bit upward or downward?
- Is your neck long and mostly vertical with a slight forward curve, or is it bent forward and flattened out?
- Are your shoulders squared up and positioned on top of your torso. or are they rounded and hanging over the front of your torso?
- Do your shoulder blades rest comfortably on your back, or do they wing out away from your body?
- Do your arms hang straight down from your shoulders, or do they hang a little forward or backward?
- Is your torso upright and vertical with a slight outward curve in your mid-back, or is your upper back rounded and your chest a bit sunken?
- Is your abdomen tucked in and flat, or does it protrude forward?
- Is there a very slight forward curve in your low back, just above your hips, or is it noticeably curved forward? Is your low back flat?
- Are your hips level with the floor or do they tip forward or backward?
- Are your legs slightly bent or are they straight and locked at the knee?
- Do both edges your feet rest similarly on the floor, or is there more weight on the inside or outside of one or both feet?

Ideally, when looking from the side, you want to see alignment: your ear canal opening, mid-shoulder, hip joint, back of knee cap, and front of ankle are all in a straight line, with your spine showing subtle forward curves in the neck and low back and a subtle backward curve in the mid-back. Again, few completely achieve this ideal posture, but tuck this image away for future reference. The idea for now is simply to observe your posture.

Body Awareness:
The Experiential Approach to Posture

Have you ever watched an infant playing with its feet? The kid clearly has no idea that the wiggly toes and pudgy feet that they find so fascinating are connected to their body. Young children haven't yet developed a sense of body awareness — a combination of their sense of touch, information about their position in space from the vestibular system, and the internal feel for where and how their bodies are currently arranged.

That sense of how your body is arranged is known as proprioception. Sometimes called "the sixth sense," proprioception collects information from your muscles and joints to give you an internal sense of how your body is positioned in space. This lets you do tasks like touching your nose with your eyes closed or walking up a staircase without having to watch every step.

Your proprioceptive system reports regularly on your body's position as you work at your desk all day. However, whether the rest of your body systems receive and act on these reports is not a sure thing. Just as your sense of smell will eventually ignore a persistent odor, your sense of proprioception will eventually ignore a constant, repetitive input. So, over time, your proprioceptive system can become habituated to the awkward postures that can result from office work. Your misguided body can begin to think that forward-head, round-shouldered, slouching posture is "normal." To remind yourself and your proprioceptive system what normal, natural posture looks and feels like, cultivate your body awareness.

Kids develop their body awareness by hurling themselves into the world and interacting with their environment in every possible way — touching, hugging, fighting, playing, running, tumbling, swinging on monkey bars, climbing trees, balancing on curbs as they walk down the street. Their frenetic approach to life lets children quickly develop a feel for where their bodies end and the rest of the world begins.

Fortunately, we internalize much of this early kinesthetic learning and carry it with us throughout our lives. Unfortunately, as we settle into adulthood and spend more time in repetitive and sedentary pursuits we begin to lose some of our feel for our bodies.

111

Without the regular stimulation of a variety of physical interactions with the world, our sense of body awareness begins to atrophy.

You need not revert to childhood to reconnect with your body. You can cultivate awareness of your grown up, office worker body by simply activating and observing the three systems that constitute body awareness.

Nurture Your Sense of Touch

Your skin is your body's largest organ, the place that physically connects you with the rest of the world. So it is no surprise that your sense of touch figures prominently in body awareness. Simply being touched or touching another person can reduce stress, improve mood, promote compassion, reduce depression, and bolster immune system function. Western cultures, especially in North America, are notoriously touch deprived, so we don't get these benefits often enough. Neither do we get the physical, kinesthetic feedback that touch contributes to our sense of body awareness. Fortunately, the remedy is close at hand. Hug a friend. Hold hands with your partner (better yet, give each other a foot massage). Hold your daughter in your lap as you read to her. Cuddle with your pet. Get a professional massage. Every time you are touched or touch someone, you enhance your sense of body awareness.

Activate your Vestibular Balance System

The best way to activate your vestibular system is to disrupt it. All kinds of fancy gadgets are available to help you challenge your vestibular system, but you don't need a stability ball or a wobble board to improve your balance. Simply standing with a narrow stance, standing on one leg, or standing with your eyes closed can make you more aware of your physical position in the world. So can walking on sand or hiking on uneven terrain. Anything you can do to discombobulate your balance and then regain it stimulates your vestibular system.

Reset Your Proprioceptive System

You can apply the postural observations you made in the previous section to cross-check your posture against the ideals, moving one body part at a time into its optimal position. This is easier said than done, of course, so the next section presents some visualizations to help guide you through one approach this.

Visualizations to Improve Your Posture

As I studied posture and talked about it with my clients over the years, I discovered and developed a number of visualizations to help them develop body awareness and improve posture. Although they aren't always 100% anatomically and physiologically accurate, visualizations can give you an accessible tool for breaking out of your habitual posture patterns. We can all benefit from a proprioceptive reset, and visualizations can help to jumpstart that reset.

So let's take a body-awareness posture tour. Start at the top of your head and work down your body to the bottom of your feet.

Why start at the head and work down the body? Doesn't it make as much sense to start at the feet and work upward? You can make a strong case for working from the feet up, using the architectural analogy of beginning with the foundation and working your way up the body structure. I have, in fact, used this model myself — and you are welcome to upend this suggested sequence and proceed bottom-up.

I now think it makes more sense to start at the top and work down though, because many postural problems associated with computer work begin as your eyes peer forward into the monitor, and because the main sensory systems that guide your posture are all in your head:

- Your vision system strives to keep your eyes level with the horizon at all times.
- The vestibular system in your inner ear helps you maintain your balance and provides information about your body's location in space.

- Your brain processes and integrates all of the information coming from the rest of your body about where you are in space.

So we'll start at the head — where so much important postural physiology happens — and work our way down your body.

These visualizations aren't presented as the be-all and end-all of postural education. The are simply one more way to help you develop more body awareness and perhaps give you some comfort and pain relief as you find more ease in your body at work.

By the way, because your body is habituated to office posture, repositioning your body with these visualization exercises may feel odd at first. But with repetition and practice your proprioceptive system can re-learn to accept and embrace posture closer to optimal.

Balance Your Bowling Ball on the Broomstick

Picture your head as a bowling ball, a children's model that weighs about ten pounds. Now imagine it balanced on top of a broomstick. The relationship between your head and neck isn't actually quite as precarious as this, but the image is not too far off the mark.

The point of this visualization is to picture the disproportionately large force create by a relatively minor displacement of your head on top of your neck. One of my massage teachers estimates that, for each inch that it goes forward, your head feels ten pounds heavier, so if your head is only one inch forward of its natural position it effectively doubles in weight, making the muscles on the back of your neck and down into your shoulders work double-time.

You can put your "bowling ball" back where it belongs a couple of different ways. The first method is to place the middle and index fingers of your dominant hand on your chin and firmly push your head straight back, picturing it sliding back like a drawer shutting. The second method is to find the knob at the base of your skull, gently grab a tuft of hair just above it, and pull upward and backward. In both cases, you'll feel your chin tuck down and the back of your head rise up as your head retracts backward. Both of these methods let you feel what it's like to put your head back over the broomstick, reducing the strain on your neck and shoulder muscles.

114

Open Your Opera Singer's Windpipe Hose

Now let's expand the picture of your neck to account for its flexibility and hollowness. In addition to the bony spine (the broomstick that holds up your bowling ball), your neck contains your esophagus and trachea. A few years ago a singer in the touring Broadway cast of "Oklahoma" came in for a massage. Our conversation turned to posture, specifically head and neck positioning. He showed me a technique that he had learned from an opera singer to "open up the windpipe" to help his voice project more loudly and clearly.

The concern for singers is that head-forward posture puts a kink in the windpipe, restricting the flow of air. Get the kink out of hose, and you can sing louder and more clearly. The repositioning method that singers use is virtually identical to the pushing-your-head-back technique in the previous visualization. Instead of physically pushing back the chin with their fingers, singers simply tuck their chin a little and then use their muscles to slide their head straight back, like a drawer closing, creating a little bit of a double chin (your cue that you have closed the drawer enough). As the drawer closes, the kink in the hose is opened up, and the breath can flow freely. Go ahead and try it. Slide your head back to make a double chin — and then belt out your favorite Broadway song.

Lengthen Your Giraffe Neck

One of my favorite pieces of trivia is the fact that giraffes have the same number of bones in their neck as humans. Like us, giraffes have seven vertebrae that connect their torso to their head. Obviously, their vertebrae are larger than ours, and they have stronger and more flexible neck muscles. Nevertheless, you can use the image of the giraffe neck to lift your head up further from your trunk. The next time you feel your head jutting forward, just imagine reaching up with your giraffe neck to nibble those tasty acacia leaves high above your desk.

Un-Slump Your Shoulder Cloak

Your shoulder girdle — the assemblage of skin, muscles, bones, and other tissues that connect your torso to your arms — is like a thick,

115

multilayered cloak that drapes over the top of your torso. With typical office posture, your "cloak" slumps forward, pulled there by your head and neck as you peer into your computer monitor and by the ensuing forward slump of your torso and rib cage.

To undo this slumping posture, you can simply push your shoulder cloak back where it belongs. To do this, place your dominant hand palm down near the top of your chest with the thumb resting under one collarbone and the forefinger under the other one. As you take a big, deep breath, push your clavicles up and back, picturing that heavy cloak sliding up and over the top of your torso as you push.

As your shoulder cloak glides back over the top of your torso, you will notice a little slack in the muscles between your shoulder blades. Contract those muscles to squeeze your shoulder blades closer together, and you'll feel what it's like to have a balanced, squared-up, optimally positioned shoulder girdle.

Lengthen Your Soup Ladle

The structures that hold up your shoulder girdle cloak are your spine and rib cage. You can picture the two of them together as a sort of inverted soup ladle. Your rib cage is the bowl of the ladle and your spine is the handle. Unlike the typical soup ladle handle, though, this one can lengthen and shorten, like a telescope. When you sit at a desk all day, your ladle bowl is pulled forward and downward under the weight of your shoulder cloak and your ladle handle (your spine) shortens as gravity pulls your head and torso toward the floor. To undo this pattern, take a big, deep breath and picture the handle of your ladle lengthening and lifting the bowl of your ladle upward as you inhale.

Squeeze Your Water Balloon

Down at bottom of this avalanching cascade of your slumping shoulder cloak and collapsing soup ladle is your abdomen. As the squishiest, least skeletally supported part of your body, your belly is at high risk of being crushed under the weight of the structures above it. You can reduce that risk by picturing your abdomen as a water balloon. Just as you can squeeze a water balloon in the middle to lengthen it, you can engage your deep abdominal muscles to restore your abdomen to its normal, un-crushed volume. Simply pull your belly button back toward your spine and hold it there for 30 seconds or so. You can do this in any posture (sitting, standing, walking), at any time (even in a meeting or on an airplane). As you pull your belly button in, picture the bottom of your abdominal water balloon pushing down into your pelvis and the top of it pushing up into your torso. Not coincidentally, running along the back of your water balloon is the lower part of that same telescoping soup ladle that holds up your torso. With this in mind, you can picture your longer, narrower, taller water balloon further lengthening your soup ladle handle.

Level Your Pelvic Bowl

Pelvis comes from the Latin for basin or Greek for bowl. Stand with your feet about hip-width apart and bend your knees a bit. Then, put your hands on your hips and picture your pelvic bowl filled to the brim with water. Gently tip it a little forward, letting a little imaginary water slosh out, and then tip it a little backward. Then bend one knee so that your pelvis drops a little to that side, and then to the other side, picturing a little water sloshing out on each side. You can also swivel your hips to draw circles in the air with your pelvis, trying to keep your pelvic bowl as level as possible as you circle both clockwise and counterclockwise. Then, still with your hands on your hips, sway your hips side to side like a hula dancer and feel your pelvic bowl rock side-to-side. Now return your focus to the front-to-back tilt and let your pelvic bowl come to rest in the middle, at a comfortable, neutral position, picturing the water level and calm.

Let Your Legs Hang Down to Your Feet

We tend to think of our legs as tree trunks rising up from our feet, but you can also think of them as vines hanging down from your hips. Standing with your feet about hip-width apart, imagine that you are a marionette, your upper body hovering effortlessly in the air and your legs dangling from your hips. First, feel the easy length in your legs and wiggle them around a bit, appreciating the relaxed connection between your hips and your ankles. Then let a little of your body weight settle down onto your knees. Push your knees

117

backward to lock them out, and then bend them a bit and gently bounce up and down. Move back and forth a few times between the locked-out knee position and the gentle bouncing and then settle into a position halfway between. Your knees will be engaged but not locked, like a sturdy vine hanging from a lush jungle tree.

Sway with the Tide from Your Ankles

Now shift your visualization from the jungle to the sea. Stand with your feet a few inches apart. Then, picture your legs as strands of kelp that are anchored to the ocean floor at your ankles. Let your knees, hips, torso, arms, shoulders, and head gently sway in the ocean currents. Focus your awareness on your ankle joints and on the subtle front-to-back, side-to-side, and circular movements happening in them. Do this for a few minutes, with your eyes both open and closed (if you wobble when you close your eyes, make sure you have a sturdy support at hand). Finally, picture the water calming to complete stillness and your body effortlessly rising straight up from your ankles, lifted by the buoyancy of your body above.

Suction-Cup Your Feet to the Floor

Just as kelp moors itself to the ocean bottom with a strong holdfast, you can anchor your posture by picturing your feet firmly attached to the floor. This visualization turns the bottoms of your feet into suction cups. Ideally, you want to do this one in bare feet, but you can benefit even if you keep your shoes on.

Stand with your feet about hip-width apart. Lean back on your heels a bit and reach forward with your toes, planting the pads at the base your toes firmly into the floor. Now lift up on those pads and reach back with your heels, making your feet as long as possible as you settle your heels back onto the floor. Now roll your feet inward, resting your weight on your heel and your big toe, and reach out to the side with your little toes. Then roll your feet outward just a bit so that your weight rests on your heel and the base of your small toes; then reach inward with your big toes. You should now feel a triangle on the bottom of each foot with points at the base of your little toe, the base of your big toe, and your heel. Finally, picture the middle of each foot lifting up, creating a suction cup that firmly sticks your feet to the floor (sort of like trying to palm a basketball with the bottom of your foot).

* * *

You may, of course, reverse this sequence; that is, root yourself first, then sway in the ocean, swing in the jungle, and work your way back up to your bowling ball. Or you can linger on any one of those visualizations to become better acquainted with that part of your body. The visualizations are intended to be just one more way to develop your body awareness.

High-Tech Postural Awareness

Years ago, I came up with an idea for a gadget to correct head-forward posture. You would wear sensor-equipped earrings on your ears and epaulets on your shoulders to detect when your head moved too far forward. The gadget would vibrate when it detected your ears in front of your shoulders to remind you to tuck your head back into place. This idea has many problems, most notably the obvious fashion-related issues, so it never went anywhere. Luckily, product designers much more clever and capable than I are at work in this area.

Scientists use all kinds of fancy equipment when they study posture: real-time 3-D X-rays, fMRIs, force plates, accelerometers, and sophisticated posture measuring garments. Physical therapists and other clinicians use such tools as goniometers, tape measures, and inclinometers to measure anatomical relationships and angles. Researchers and clinicians use photography and videography to monitor posture in real time and to track changes over time.

Some of this technology is finding its way into consumer products that can help you monitor and improve your posture at work right now. The companies Lumo and iPosture both offer tiny, wearable devices that ingeniously monitor your posture and alert you with a gentle vibration when you slump or slouch. Nekoze for the Mac, Posture Trainer for Android, and other apps use your computer's built-in camera to watch your posture and alert you when you slouch. Philips sells a computer display monitor called the ErgoSensor that includes a camera that monitors your posture and your ergonomic set-up (as of this writing, the ErgoSensor is available only in Europe). New gadgets like these are launched all the time, often beginning as a Kickstarter crowdfunding project.

In the not-too-distant future, we will see even more sophisticated posture-monitoring devices. Clever computer programmers are already writing apps for Microsoft's Kinect controller to help optimize your posture at a computer. The company Leap Motion makes a motion-sensitive game controller that can also be used in posture applications. Companies that make "smart garments" draw huge crowds at consumer electronics shows, and wearable technology is one of the biggest trends mentioned at technology and start-up events. So keep your eye on the tech news to watch for even more posture-monitoring gear.

Developing Better Posture Habits

Remember: Posture is among the most hard-wired parts of your behavior, so be extra diligent and allow plenty of time to cultivate new posture habits.

Add a Tiny Habit

Recall B.J. Fogg's recipe for a Tiny Habit: After I [existing habit/anchor], I will [new tiny behavior]. You might try some of the following ideas:

- After I turn on my computer monitor, I will tuck my chin down and lift up the back of my head as I retract it backwards.
- After I open my email program, I will place my thumb under one clavicle and forefinger under the other and push my "shoulder cloak" up and back.
- After I sit down in my chair, I will tuck my belly button back toward my spine and hold it there for 30 seconds.
- After I stand up, I will sway my hips a bit to feel my pelvic bowl.
- After I arrive at the printer, I will balance standing on one leg while the printing job finishes.

120

- After I arrive at the copy machine, I will lock and and then flex my knees to find the comfortable engaged position in between.
- After I walk into my office and close the door, I will plant my feet on the floor and let my body sway like ocean kelp for 30 seconds.
- After I observe a poor posture in someone else, I will immediately embody the opposite in myself.
- As I walk past a window, mirror, or other reflective surface, I will glance at my posture and note any areas for improvement.

Modify a Habit Loop

Recall Charles Duhigg's habit loop and how you can manipulate each part of it — the cue, the routine, and the reward — as well as the underlying craving. Some ideas:

- The classic office posture is the "slouch." The cue is the setting — your office chair and desk. You sit down, reach for your computer, peer into your monitor, and immediately become engrossed in your work. If you do this routine without conscious attention to your posture, you settle into the classic slouch: your shoulders hunched forward and your hips rolled backward, your normally upright spine collapsing into a C-shaped vestige of its former self. The reward is the temporary "comfort" you get from moving into a new position. This is one habit loop that's definitely worth modifying, so see if you can find a new routine that involves a more upright posture.
- A classic relaxation routine for stressed-out office workers is to sit down in front of the TV after a long day at the office. The cue is the end of the workday, the routine is turning on the TV and plopping onto the couch, and the reward is some relaxation and entertainment. There are many other routines that could replace the TV viewing, but a great one that can help cultivate your body awareness is getting a professional massage. In addition to helping you get in touch — literally — with your body, massage can help reduce any office aches and pains you may have, and it is a proven stress reducer. You don't have to get one every day (as the famous entertainer Bob

Hope did for his entire adult life), but replacing your TV routine with a massage once a week is a great posture-enhancing ritual.

- If you're one of the many office workers (especially those who work at home or in other casual environments) who routinely sit with crossed legs, sit on their feet, or otherwise twist their lower bodies in relation to their upper bodies, it's worth examining that habit loop. The cue is likely a quest for comfort, or it may be a carry-over habit from another context (for example, the way you studied as a student), You may just be fidgety. Your routine is sitting in the desired position. The reward may be satisfaction of your craving for familiarity or relief from your fidgetiness. In any position, whether with crossed legs or with your legs are tucked under you, don't stay stationary for long stretches. One possible solution is to find other cues that prompt you to change positions more regularly. Another is to mix up the routine so that sit in the same position no longer than 20 minutes.

Adopt a Practice

Because posture is such a deep habit, it is often best to address it indirectly, to perform practices that include a strong posture component. Any number of practices can help you consciously engage with your body and improve your posture. Here are a few posture-practice ideas:

- My favorite posture guru is Esther Gokhale (pronounced GO-clay). Her "Gokhale Method" helps you return to a natural way of moving, what she calls "primal posture.
- Modern yoga developed out of ancient traditions; cultivating a yoga practice can help you return to natural, pre-office-work posture.
- Tai chi is another ancient tradition that can help reverse desk posture. Tai chi is perhaps best known nowadays as a proven fall preventer for seniors, but it can help anyone at any age develop balance, body awareness, and better posture.
- Pilates was originally developed as a fitness regimen in a World War I prisoner of war camp. After Joseph Pilates moved to New York, professional dancers discovered his

method, which is how the practice became associated with good posture.

- The Feldenkrais Method and the Alexander Technique each take an approach that focuses on improving your body awareness so that you can perform day-to-day activities gracefully and naturally, with good posture.
- Taking up a sport that requires a lot of balance — gymnastics, ice hockey, or horseback riding — can, of course, help your posture. So can a sport that emphasizes good postural form, such as rowing or weightlifting.
- Any form of dance — ballet, modern, jazz, ballroom, social, and traditional ethnic dance — will boost up your body awareness several notches, and it's lots of fun.

Take a Plunge

Go nuts! Throw a monkey wrench into your current set-up to create instant, widespread change in your posture habits. A few ideas:

- Run away and join the circus to become an acrobat, aerialist, or tightrope walker.
- Quit your job and become a competitive ballroom dancer.
- Get certified as a yoga, Pilates, or tai chi teacher.
- Take several traditional dance classes; then move to Morocco, India, Cuba, Brazil, Mali, or Ghana for a year to solidify your skills. Finally, return home and share your moves by teaching classes.

Suggested Reading

8 Steps to a Pain-Free Back: Natural Posture Solutions for Pain in the Back, Neck, Shoulder, Hip, Knee, and Foot, Esther Gokhale and Susan Adams

Sources

"Position Yourself to Stay Well: The Right Body Alignment Can Help You Avoid Falls and Prevent Muscle and Joint Pain." Consumer Reports on Health, February 1, 2006.

"Proprioception." Wikipedia, the Free Encyclopedia, September 12, 2013. http://en.wikipedia.org/

Briñol, Pablo, Richard E. Petty, and Benjamin Wagner. "Body Posture Effects on Self-Evaluation: A Self-Validation Approach." European Journal of Social Psychology 39, no. 6 (October 2009): 1053–64.

Carney, Dana R., Amy J. C. Cuddy, and Andy J. Yap. "Power Posing: Brief Nonverbal Displays Affect Neuroendocrine Levels and Risk Tolerance." Psychological Science 21, no. 10 (October 1, 2010): 1363–68.

Cuddy, Amy JC, Caroline Ashley Wilmuth, and Dana R. Carney. "The Benefit of Power Posing before a High-Stakes Social Evaluation," 2012. http://dash.harvard.edu/

Egoscue, Pete. Pain Free at Your PC. Bantam, 2009.

Egoscue, Pete. Pain Free: A Revolutionary Method for Stopping Chronic Pain. Bantam, 2014.

Ehtemam, F., P.A Forbes, AC. Schouten, F. C T Van der Helm, and R. Happee. "Galvanic Vestibular Stimulation Elicits Consistent Head #x2013;Neck Motion in Seated Subjects." IEEE Transactions on Biomedical Engineering 59, no. 7 (July 2012): 1978–84.

Gokhale, Esther, and Susan Adams. 8 Steps to a Pain-Free Back: Natural Posture Solutions for Pain in the Back, Neck, Shoulder, Hip, Knee, and Foot. 1 edition. Stanford, CA: Pendo Press, 2008.

Huang, L., A. D. Galinsky, D. H. Gruenfeld, and L. E. Guillory. "Powerful Postures Versus Powerful Roles: Which Is the Proximate Correlate of Thought and Behavior?" Psychological Science 22, no. 1 (January 1, 2011): 95–102.

Strack, Fritz, Leonard L. Martin, and Sabine Stepper. "Inhibiting and Facilitating Conditions of the Human Smile: A Nonobtrusive Test of the Facial Feedback Hypothesis." Journal of Personality and Social Psychology 54, no. 5 (1988): 768.

This is a partial list of sources consulted as I wrote this chapter, including only items mentioned or referred to above. For a full list of everything I read as I prepared this chapter, please visit sitless.com/chapter5

Chapter 6
Exercise for Office-Work Patterns

When you think about fitness, the first thing that likely comes to mind is exercise. Why, then, does this chapter come last?

First, for longevity and overall health, the NEAT routine-movement habits that you began to develop when reading Chapter 3 are arguably more important than any specific exercise. Remember, the research findings about the deadliness of prolonged sedentary behavior are crystal clear. Simply getting out of your chair and moving regularly is probably the most immediately beneficial thing you can do for your physical health at work. Routine, non-exercise movement trumps exercise.

Second, for your physical comfort and well-being in the office, what you learned from the chapters on posture and ergonomics merit the top position in your office fitness plan. Those are your ongoing day-to-day, hour-to-hour, minute-to-minute concerns. If your posture suffers or your ergonomic set-up gets out of whack, you will definitely feel it. Posture and ergonomics provide the physical infrastructure for your health at work, giving your body the internal and external support it needs to work pain-free eight hours a day. Postural awareness and regular ergonomic self-check-ups trump exercise.

That said, exercise is still a vital component of your office fitness plan, just as it is the foundation of any fitness program. It can both prepare you for the unexpected physical challenges of office work, helping you get fit for work. And it can give you another healthy and productive reason to take regular breaks from your office routine, helping you get fit at work.

And you are, of course, familiar with the list of well-documented, time-tested reasons for a regular exercise routine. It makes you stronger, more flexible, more aerobically fit, and steadier on your feet. Regular exercise is a proven path to a longer lifespan and reduced disease risk. And when your body is more robust, you are better able to handle the vicissitudes of life, like sprinting to catch an early arriving bus.

The Benefits of Exercise

In fact, there's a whole laundry list of good reasons to exercise. Regular exercise can help you:

- Bolster your brain health and cognitive prowess
- Boost your creativity
- Improve your memory
- Enhance your learning ability
- Reduce your stress and anxiety levels
- Improve your mood (from run-of-the-mill contentment to a full-on "runner's high")
- Sleep better
- Manage your weight
- Improve your bone health
- Improve your muscle tone and mass
- Improve your heart and cardiovascular health
- Reduce your risk of diseases like cancer, diabetes, and stroke
- Reduce your risk of Alzheimer's disease and other forms of dementia
- Boost your energy level and increase your sense of vitality
- Better tolerate pain
- Reduce your risk of falling
- Get you outdoors
- Lengthen your life
- Add some fun to your life

How Much Exercise Do You Need?

How much must you exercise to garner these benefits? The U.S. Government's 2008 Physical Activity Guidelines recommend 2-1/2 hours of moderately intense or 1-1/4 hours of vigorous aerobic physical activity each week, spread over several days to prevent overuse injuries. These recommendations let you mix and match your exercise, proportionally dividing up moderate and vigorous activities. The guidelines also recommend two days per week of moderate- to high-intensity strengthening routines that work all of the major muscle groups. They also note that any activity is better than inactivity.

The U.S. Centers for Disease Control and Prevention points out that you need not do all of a day's exercise at once. It's fine to break up your routines into bouts of as little as 10 minutes of exercise at a time, taking three 10-minute walks instead of one 30-minute walk, for example. This is great news for us time-challenged office workers.

The government recommendations are for base levels of fitness to keep you hale and hearty in the short term and help you head off disease over the long term. To move beyond this maintenance level of fitness — to prepare for athletic activities or look more fit in your swimming suit or wedding dress — you'll have to do more. To get stronger, you'll need to do progressively more difficult strength exercises. To train for a marathon, you'll have to run progressively longer distances. To become an acrobat, you'll have to do progressively more difficult balancing feats.

To be precise about how much and how vigorously you exercise, you can use fancy heart-rate monitors and activity trackers, but that's not really necessary. Several research studies have shown that simply jotting down what you do and paying attention to how difficult an exercise seems is nearly as accurate as these gadgets. Your own subjective rating of perceived exertion (RPE) can help you identify an activity as light (little to no difficulty), moderate (an activity that gets you sweating but still lets you carry on a conversation), or vigorous (labored breath but brief bursts of conversation still possible).

By the way, some intriguing research suggests that even less exercise than is currently recommended can still reap disease prevention and cardiovascular health benefits. Duck-chul Lee and his colleagues (2014) reported similar benefits from running longer distances and running as little as 5 to 10 minutes a day. The British newspaper The Telegraph reported on in-progress research by Canadian researcher Martin Gibala that shows the benefits of very brief (as little as one minute a day a few times a week) bouts of high-intensity exercise. This ongoing research is by no means conclusive, but it does hint at the power of doing any amount of exercise. Don't replace your conventional workouts with these practices just yet, but do keep this research in mind when you have time for only a brief workout.

Principles of Exercise Science

Few industries are as vulnerable to fads and trends as the exercise business. From Ab Roller gadgets to Zumba workouts, from 19th Century massage belts to modern "whole body vibration systems," from Suzzanne Somers' Thighmaster to the Shake Weight, from Jack LaLanne to Richard Simmons, from Charles Atlas to Timothy Ferris — there has never been a shortage of exercise gear, gimmicks, workout systems, and advice.

You might hope that scientific research and the media's coverage of it would keep us well informed and keep the exercise industry honest. Don't count on it. In an edifying and enjoyable New York Times op-ed column, Daniel Duane observes that exercise researchers "rarely research the practical questions you and I want answered, like which workout routine is best." They do tons of great research, of course, but it is typically on very focused and specific areas, the results of which are rarely portrayed in dispassionate, objective reports. "The problem," says Duane, "Is that everybody in the fitness industry grabs onto this basic science and then twists the results to come up with something that sounds like a science-backed recommendation for whatever they're selling."

Then who can you listen to? Fortunately, athletic culture has given rise to a body of research that has been articulated as a set of principles that can guide your exercise plan. Here's what scientists, scholars, trainers, and coaches have discovered about exercise:

You Are Unique

Your genetic endowment, interest in different activities, history of injury, and experience with physical fitness and athletics are all unique to you. Your exercise goals are unique to your situation and circumstances. Your ability to enjoy, tolerate, undertake, or attempt exercise depends on hundreds of factors unique to you. Your preference for different kinds of workouts and activities should always guide your exercise routines. This is the principle of *individual differences*.

Increase the Difficulty

To make any fitness gains — to be able to run farther and faster, move more weight, become more flexible, develop better balance — you have to challenge your body with increasingly difficult workouts. This is the principle of *overload* or *diminishing returns*.

Pace Yourself

To avoid exhaustion, pain, and injury, you need to rest and recover between workouts. You can't just constantly do more and more difficult workouts. Developing physical fitness is a gradual process. This is the principle of *progression*.

Shake Things Up

Your body quickly adapts to new activities and becomes adept at executing them. In athletic activities like hitting a baseball or propelling a scull, doing the same activity over and over helps you develop coordination, proficiency, and even sublime grace. However, the efficiency of motion that you gain from that repetition may no longer challenge your body, causing you to plateau at a level of achievement lower than you'd like. You can ascend to the next level by breaking up your routines. This is the principle of *variation* or *adaptation*.

Use It or Lose It

Unfortunately, those adaptions can easily be undone. Your muscles atrophy when you stop using them. Your joints grow creakier and stiffer when you stop moving them. Your aerobic fitness declines as soon as you stop running. Your steadiness on your feet suffers when you sit on your butt all day. This is the principle of *reversibility* or *use/disuse*.

Be Specific

If you want to be able to run faster, you have to strengthen your running muscles. If you want to ride your bicycle through the Alps, you have to develop your biking skills. To develop any particular skill or ability, you must train specifically for that activity. If your goal is general fitness rather than proficiency in a specific sport, then cross-training and other non-focused training activities are fine, but to do one thing well, you must focus on it. This is the principle of *specificity*.

* * *

Scientists, teachers, and trainers might cite other principles as well, but every principle I have encountered can fit under one of those above. Regardless of its comprehensiveness, with the variety of practices and advice out there, it can be helpful to have a scientifically vetted list like this guiding your exercise routines.

An Exercise Plan for Office Workers

When you consider the sedentary, stationary, ergonomic, and postural challenges of office work discussed earlier in this book, your exercise path becomes clear. You need to do more activities that get you moving in general and that specifically pull you up out of your forward-slouched desk posture.

Just as baseball pitchers balance their workouts by doing two or three times as much exercise on their non-pitching muscles, you can benefit both from developing the muscles that do the work of positioning you at your desk and operating your computer and from developing even more the supporting cast of muscles that hold you upright and move you around.

The Goals of Any Exercise Program

The goals of exercise are to help you develop strength, endurance, flexibility, and stability.

These goals complement one other. You need flexibility to get all of the strengthening benefits of a full squat. You need to have aerobic endurance to strengthen your legs for a marathon. You need strength to keep your balance as you bicycle on uneven terrain. You need stability on your feet and strength in your core to lift heavy weights.

This complementarity explains the growing popularity of "functional," full-body workouts like MovNat and CrossFit. Functional workouts are much more natural than the gadget-oriented exercise routines that arose in the mid-20th Century. Machine-oriented workouts from that era — like the Nautilus circuit training system, which remains popular to this day — were a great business model for both bottom-line-oriented gym owners and busy, efficiency-minded exercisers. But the focus of these systems on isolating specific muscle groups resulted in fit-looking people who weren't necessarily fit.

Functional fitness routines return us to more natural exercise routines that prepare us for real-life physical activities. Whether you want to be able to pick up your kids and carry groceries in from the car or sprint for an early-arriving bus, functional workouts promise the old-fashioned fitness levels that helped us survive and thrive in more physically challenging times.

As useful as functional routines are, however, exercises and workouts that focus on specific body regions are still valuable — especially for office workers like you. Sometimes you need to focus on a neglected or abused body area to prepare it to resume its role in your fully functioning body. So you will benefit from balanced workouts that include both functional routines and occupation-specific exercises.

The Goals of an Office Fitness Exercise Program

To function well in your desk job, you need an exercise plan that addresses the unique physical challenges of working in an office.

Remember the "shoulder cloak" described in the posture chapter? Cultivating postural awareness is just one way to pull your "cloak" back to where it belongs. You can also do exercises that mobilize and release the muscles on the front of your shoulder girdle and strengthen and engage the muscles on the back of it. This same approach can help undo patterns like the head-forward posture, a slouching C-shaped spine, and sitting-induced chronic hip flexion.

In fact, exercise can help rectify a whole laundry list of office-work imbalance patterns. This table lists some of those patterns and the muscles that you can release and engage to address them. If you haven't studied anatomy, some of these muscle names and other terms may be unfamiliar to you, but you need no anatomy knowledge to address these work patterns.

Summary of Office Work Patterns

Pattern	*Release*	*Engage*
head forward	SCM, anterior neck	posterior neck
chin up	suboccipitals	longus capitis
scapula up and over	pectoralis minor	lower trapezius
scapula protracted	serratus anterior	mid-trap, rhomboid
shoulders forward	pecs, ant. deltoid	lats, post. deltoid
shoulder int. rot.	subscapularis	infrasp./teres minor
arm flexion	biceps, arm flexors	triceps
forearm pronation	pronator teres	supinator
forearm flexion	forearm flexors	forearm extensors
rigid thorax	deep thorax muscles	deep thorax muscles
torso collapse	deep posture muscles	transv. ab., "core"
C-shaped spine	abs, pecs, serr. ant.	erector spinae
trunk flexion	abs, psoas	erector spinae, lats
hip flexion	iliopsoas, hip flexors	glutes, hamstrings
flexed upper leg	hamstrings	quads
flexed lower leg	gastroc., soleus	tibialis anterior
plantar shortening	foot flexors	foot extensors

The next section sets out some exercises that specifically address those patterns. Also, your personal trainer should be familiar with all of the affected muscles and can show you other exercises and help you design other workouts that address these patterns.

The terms release and engage in this table are placeholder terms to describe a number of possible muscular actions. **Release** refers to any exercise or other measure intended to relax or lengthen a muscle or muscle group — passive stretching, active stretching (PNF stretching, Active Isolated Stretching, etc.), reciprocal inhibition as an antagonist muscle contracts, self-myofascial release (SMR), self-massage, professional massage, postural awareness, etc. **Engage** refers to any exercise or other measure intended to put a muscle or muscle group to work — typically using a muscle to move your body or a weight against gravity or other form of resistance.

In normal, natural, day-to-day movements like walking, running, jumping, or lifting, you constantly both release and engage multiple pairs of muscles and muscle groups. In the office, you are stuck in static postures doing repetitive motions. That is why it is crucial to do both functional workouts to reengage those natural muscle pairings and targeted exercises that specifically release posturally shortened muscles and engage their opposing counterparts.

Since office work generally pulls your head and shoulders forward and flexes your torso and trunk and legs, you want to bias your workouts toward exercises that pull you the opposite way. Like baseball pitchers who spend twice as much time working on their non-pitching muscles, you want to emphasize exercises that pull your shoulders and head back and that pull your torso and trunk and legs upright. The next section shows you some exercises that specifically address office-work patterns; and the following sections describe:

- **no-sweat exercises** you can do right at your desk or in a break room
- **stealth exercises** you can do in meetings, conference sessions, or on airplanes
- **fun exercises** to make sure you remember to keep a smile on your face as you improve your office fitness.

These suggested exercises and workouts are by no means the be-all and end-all of office-fitness exercise. I encourage you and your personal trainer to draw on your own ideas and backgrounds to come up with even more creative ways to get you moving.

A Note on Exercise Safety

Consult your physician before embarking on any new exercise program. Then observe all of the usual exercise safety conventions: always warm up, use the right gear, practice good form, work out in a safe environment, recruit a spotter if you aren't 100% certain that you can manage a piece of equipment yourself, stay adequately hydrated, etc. Stop exercising if you feel any pain or distress.

Exercises for Office Work Patterns

Here are some exercises to help you begin to address those office-work patterns. The printed page is not the best place to teach exercises, so I offer below a brief description exercise of one simple exercise you can do to start to counteract each pattern. I also include for each pattern a link to a web page with more detailed explanations and examples of other exercises you can do to further address the pattern.

Head Forward and Chin Up Patterns

As you peer forward into your computer monitor, your head is drawn forward, just is it is drawn toward the windshield of your car on a foggy night. As the muscles on the front of your neck pull your head forward, the muscles on the back of your neck are drawn taut. As your head goes forward, your body also instinctively pulls the back of your head downward to bring your eyes back up so that they are level with the horizon. The result is head-forward posture and an upwardly tilted chin. To counteract this pattern, do exercises that retract your head.

The quickest, simplest way to **retract your head** is to:

- tuck your chin down,
- lift up the back of your head, and
- slide your head backward as if you were closing a file drawer.

This pulls your head back so that it is once again centered over your body's mid-line.

More head-retraction exercises:
http://sitless.com/exercises/head-retraction/

Neck Stiffness Pattern

The consequences of head-forward posture ripple down to displace and irritate the muscles that rotate, flex, and extend your neck, resulting in a stiff neck. To counteract this pattern, do exercises that get your neck moving again.

Neck Rotation

Your neck turns best when it is properly positioned, so to **rotate your neck**:

- tuck your chin back to retract your head,
- keep your head level throughout the rotation (don't tuck or lift your chin), and
- rotate your head as far as you can to one side, then the other.

At the end of each turn, try to rotate one or two degrees more at the end of the motion. Rotate only your neck and head, not your shoulders and torso.

Neck Flexion

Of the two kinds of neck flexion, the first is flexing the very deep muscles on the front of your neck to tuck your chin down; that is part of the head retraction routine described above. The second kind of flexion involves bending the whole neck forward from its base on top of the torso.

The simplest way to **exercise your neck flexors** is to:

- lie on your back with your knees bent and your feet flat on the floor,
- tuck in your chin, and
- lift your head off of the floor.

Neck Lateral Flexion

The simplest way to **laterally flex your neck** is to stand up and

- tuck in your chin,
- bring your ear toward your shoulder,
- return to upright, and
- bring your ear toward your opposite shoulder.

Neck Extension

The simplest way to **extend your neck** is to stand up and

- tuck in your chin,

- roll your neck toward the back, initiating the motion at the base of your neck, where it attaches to your torso,
- look at the ceiling, and
- return to neutral.

More neck exercises:
http://sitless.com/exercises/neck/

Shoulder-Forward Pattern

One of the most troublesome office-work patterns is the forward-shoulder posture that results from reaching for a keyboard and mouse all day. To counteract this pattern, do exercises that retract your shoulders (pull them back).

The quickest and simplest way to **retract your shoulders** is to stand up and

- let your arms hang at your side,
- rotate your arms so that your palms face forward,
- lift your arms to a 45-degree angle (halfway between straight out to the side and hanging at your side)
- pinch your shoulder blades together.

Because so many moving parts are involved in the shoulder-forward pattern, your ongoing shoulder-retraction exercise routines should account for all of the components of shoulder retraction. The exercises on the sitless.com website address each part of this pattern.

More shoulder-retraction exercises:
http://sitless.com/exercises/shoulder-retraction/

Shoulder Internal Rotation Pattern

Another part of the shoulder-forward pattern is the internal rotation of the shoulder joint itself. To counteract this pattern, do exercises that externally rotate your shoulders.

The quickest and simplest way to **externally rotate your shoulder** is to stand up and

- flex your arms to a 90-degree angle with your hands facing each other,
- rotate your arms out to the side so that your palms face forward,
- pinch your shoulder blades together at the end of the motion.

Simply repeating this motion will begin to undo the internal-rotation pattern, but adding resistance to the exercise will strengthen the external shoulder rotators even more.

More shoulder rotation exercises:
`http://sitless.com/exercises/shoulder-rotation/`

Arm Flexion Pattern

Sitting at a desk and using a computer all day keeps your arms bent and gives the muscles that extend your arm — your triceps — few opportunities to move. To counteract this pattern, do exercises that engage and strengthen your triceps muscles.

The quickest, simplest way to **exercise your triceps** is to stand up and

- hold a light dumbbell or water bottle with both hands,
- with your arms over your head and your arms bent with the weight behind your head, and
- straighten your arms so that they are up over your head, keeping your arms next to your ears throughout.

More arm extension exercises:
`http://sitless.com/exercises/arm-extension/`

Forearm Supination Pattern

Turning your palms downward all day to type on a keyboard results in a position called forearm pronation. To counteract this pattern, do exercises that do the opposite motion, which is called supination.

The quickest way to **engage your forearm supinators** is to

137

- tuck your upper arms in against your body,
- bend your arms to a 90-degree angle, and
- turn your palms face up.

You can add resistance to this motion by holding a light dumbbell in your hand as you supinate your forearms.

More forearm supination exercises:
http://sitless.com/exercises/forearm-supination/

Forearm Flexion Pattern

Using a keyboard and mouse all day overuses your forearm flexor muscles. To counteract this pattern, do exercises that engage your forearm extensor muscles.

The quickest, simplest way to **exercise your forearm extensors** is to

- hold a light dumbbell in each hand, palm facing downward,
- rest your forearm on a weight bench or similar surface,
- extend your wrist upward.

More forearm extension exercises:
http://sitless.com/exercises/forearm-extension/

Thoracic Immobility Pattern

After sitting, standing, slumping, slouching, or otherwise remaining stationary at a desk all day, your rib cage and the middle part of your spine begin to get stuck in place. To counteract this pattern, do exercises that get your thorax moving.

The quickest and simplest way to **get your thorax moving** again is to sit in a non-rotating chair and

squeeze a tennis ball (or something similar) between your knees (to engage your core muscles and prevent your lower back from moving),

- place your hands on top of your head,
- rotate your torso to one side, and then

138

- laterally flex your torso to the same side.
- Repeat on the other side.

More thoracic mobilization exercises:
`http://sitless.com/exercises/thoracic-mobility/`

Torso Collapse Pattern

As your upper body succumbs to the tug of gravity, your torso collapses downward. To counteract the torso-collapse pattern, do exercises that lengthen your low back. Technically, it's unlikely that you can truly lengthen your spine. However, you can improve your posture and actually become a little taller by restoring the natural curvature of your spine. You've already begun doing this with the head-retraction, neck, and thorax exercises described earlier.

The quickest and simplest way to begin to **lengthen your low back** is to stand up and

- raise both hands over your head, palms facing each other,
- take a big deep breath, and then as you exhale,
- laterally flex your body to one side, and then
- inhale as you return to vertical.
- Repeat on the other side.

This stretches the muscles on either side of your lower spine, mainly the quadratus lumborum muscle, but also the lumbar multifidi muscles and deep muscles that lie along the spine.

More low-back exercises:
`http://sitless.com/exercises/low-back-lengthening`

Trunk Flexion Pattern

The C-shaped spine that comes with prolonged slumping puts you into a persistent trunk flexion pattern. To counteract this pattern, do exercises that extend your trunk.

The quickest and simplest way to begin to **extend your trunk** is to stand up and

139

- place your hands on your hips, fingers resting on the front of your hip bones and thumbs on the back, and
- bend your upper body backwards, keeping your neck and torso long and initiating the motion in your low back.

This is a move that many office workers do instinctively after a long spell of sitting.

More trunk-extension exercises:
http://sitless.com/exercises/trunk-extension/

Hip Flexion Pattern

Sitting all day keeps your hips perpetually flexed. To counteract this pattern, do exercises that extend your hips.

The quickest, simplest way to **extend your hips** is to stand up and

- hold onto a chair or similar support and
- engage your core so that only your legs will move, and
- extend your leg backward.
- Repeat with the other leg.

More hip extension exercises:
http://sitless.com/exercises/hip-extension/

Leg Immobility Pattern

Sitting all day takes your leg muscles completely out of their game. Adding insult to injury, the hamstring muscles on the back of your leg are crushed into your chair by the weight of your upper body. Even if you work at a standing desk, you aren't moving your legs as much as they would prefer. To counteract this pattern, do exercises that exercise your legs.

The quickest and simplest way to **exercise your legs** at work is to stand up and do a few squats. Stand with your feet about shoulder width apart and

- with your feet pointing straight ahead or just a little out to the side and
- holding your arms straight out in front of you (to stabilize your body), and
- keeping your chest up, butt out, and knees over your ankles throughout the movement,
- sit down into an imaginary chair, until your thighs are parallel to the floor, and then
- stand up.

More leg exercises:
http://sitless.com/exercises/leg/

No-Sweat Exercises

Since you spend most of your day in the office, you need to learn some exercises you can do there. You can do all of these exercises right in your office — at your desk or in a break room, an empty conference room, or a stairwell— with only minimal equipment and without breaking a sweat.

Each exercise is briefly described here. More complete descriptions, videos, and other guidance are available at the sitless.com website. If an exercise is new to you, you might also want to consult your personal trainer or another exercise expert.

Endurance

- Run up a few flights of stairs, taking them two or three at a time.
- Run in place like a football player for 30-60 seconds, bringing your knees as high as possible with each step.
- Try to kick your butt with your heel, alternating legs, for 30-60 seconds.
- Do 20-30 jumping jacks, either full jumping jacks (clapping your hands over your head) or half (raising your arms as high as your shoulders).
- Do 10-15 four-count burpees: 1) drop into a squat with your hands on the ground, 2) kick your feet back, keeping your

hands on the floor and your arms straight, 3) immediately jump back to the squat position, and 4) jump up back to standing.

- Shadow box vigorously for a 30- to 60-second round
- Do walk lunges around your office or in an empty conference room for a minute or two

Strength

- Do 10-20 body-weight squats — feet shoulder width apart, arms straight out in front (for balance), butt out, chest up, squat until thighs are parallel to floor then back to standing.
- Do 5-10 one-legged squats, sinking as shallowly or deeply as you prefer, holding onto a wall or table for support if needed.
- Do a wall sit — back against the wall, feet flat, knees bent 90 degrees — for 30-60 seconds.
- Do 10-20 leg abductions — stand on one leg and take other leg straight out to the side (hold onto your desk or a chair if needed for balance) and repeat with other leg.
- If your clothing permits and floor is an option, kneel on all fours and do thigh extensions, bending one leg at a time to 90 degrees and lifting your foot straight toward ceiling leg extension.
- Drop to the floor and do 8-15 push-ups. If you're worried about scuffing your shoes or mussing your clothes, do a modified push-up by putting your hands on your desk or another sturdy surface.
- If you have dumbbells or a couple of full water bottles handy, do 10-20 biceps curls.
- Using a sturdy, non-wheeled chair, do 10-15 dips, hands gripping the front edge of the chair shoulder width apart.
- If you have dumbbells (or a pair of heavy briefcases) handy, do 8-12 low-weight deadlifts, keeping your chest high and your butt back throughout the movement and thrusting your hips forward to finish the lift.
- Do 10-15 deep lunges, keeping your spine vertical and neutral, your forward knee directly over your ankle, and dropping the back knee straight down with each repetition.

- Do 15-10 calf raises, using the back of your chair for stability if necessary.

Flexibility and Mobility

- To open up tight hips, stand in a shallow lunge (about half the depth of a full lunge) for 30-60 seconds, squaring up your hips, sinking your weight onto your front leg, and keeping your spine vertical.
- To extend an over-flexed low back, stand with your hands on your hips and push your hips forward as you pull your shoulders back.
- To open up your chest, stand with your arms out to the side, inhaling and opening your chest as you pull your arms back, exhaling as you bring your arms forward, moving your arms through a slightly different angle with each breath
- To relax your inwardly rotated shoulders, stand with your arms bent to 90 degrees and rotate them outward as far outward as possible as you inhale, relax as you exhale, repeat 10-12 times
- Either standing up or sitting tall in your chair, reach both arms straight up over your head, alternately reaching a little higher with each arm
- Stretch your neck by letting your head hang over so that your right ear drops toward your right shoulder and then reaching up with your right hand to pull it just a little closer to your shoulder; hold for a few seconds and then repeat on the left
- Roll your shoulders forward and backward, first with your arms hanging at your side and then with your arms held straight out to the side
- Stretch your forearm muscles by reaching one arm straight out, palm up, and placing the fingers of the opposite hand in your palm and gently pulling back
- Stretch your inner thigh and hamstring muscles by standing with your feet as far apart as possible and bending forward at the waist, keeping your back straight and reaching toward the floor with your hands

Core and Stability

- If lying down on the floor is an option, do 5-10 bridges, lying on your back and slowly lifting and lowering your hips with your shoulders and head on the floor, arms on the floor with palms down, feet shoulder width apart, and legs bent to 90 degrees.
- Lying face down, do the Superman pose, reaching out and up with both arms and reaching back and up with both legs.
- Lying face down, do the diagonal Superman pose, alternately reaching out and up with one arm and back and up with the opposite leg.
- Stand on one leg and swing your other leg back and forth and side to side.
- Stand on one leg as you do anything — reading, typing, talking on the phone.
- Put a tennis ball or something similar between your knees and squeeze your knees together to engage your core muscles as you sit.
- Do a 30-60 plank and/or a side plank or other plank variation
- Do "the pencil" pose, standing with feet together and reaching straight up with your fingers interlaced, for 60-90 seconds.

Stealth Exercises

When you're stuck in a meeting, on an airplane, or in another situation where it might not be appropriate to look like you're working out, you can still sneak in some exercises. Try to keep a really blasé look on your face as you do these exercises.

- Squeeze your butt cheeks together and hold for 15-30 seconds, repeat.
- Do Kegel exercises, tightening and then holding the pelvic floor muscles (as if you were trying not to urinate), hold for 3-5 seconds and then relax for 3-5 seconds and repeat several times.
- Raise and lower your legs, one a time, under the desk or conference table, as slowly as possible.

- Surreptitiously slip a tape dispenser, tennis ball, or binder between your knees and squeeze your knees together (by the way, this exercise actually does engage your core muscles, unlike sitting on an exercise ball or wobbly chair).
- Do old-fashioned Charles Atlas-style dynamic tension exercises. Hook your hands together with curled fingers and try to pull them apart or place your palms together and push them toward one another.
- Do a chair squat. Take your time to slowly get in and out of your chair, enjoying the pleasant tension in your quads as you deliberately settle into your seat.
- Do stealth wall leans. Stand about a foot and half from a wall with your forearm casually resting on it, doing a sort of sideways push-up as you lean into and away from the wall.
- If you are standing up, stand on one leg and make small circles with your other foot both clockwise and counterclockwise.
- If you are sitting down, lift both feet off of the floor and make small circles with both feet.
- From a sitting position, straighten out one leg and draw the alphabet with your foot under the table, repeat with the other leg.
- Tuck your belly button toward your spine to engage your abdominal muscles (like the "water balloon" visualization in the posture chapter).
- Pull your shoulder blades together and hold for 15-30 seconds, repeat.

Fun Exercise Ideas

Thinking of exercise as drudgery that you perform at the gym is a sure way to perpetuate sedentary behavior. Finding fun activities that get you moving is a much better strategy. Here (on the next page) is a list to get you started. If you don't recognize the name of an exercise, just Google it.

Acrobatics	Golf	Pole Dancing
Aerials	Grappling	Qi Gong
African Dance	Gymnastics	Racewalking
Ballroom Dance	Gyrotonics	Rebounder
Barre	Hiking	Rock Climbing
Beach Volleyball	Hip-Hop Dance	Rowing
Belly Dancing	Hula Dance	Salsa Dance
Bollywood Dance	Hula Hoop	Samba Dance
Bootcamp Workouts	Ice Skating	Skateboarding
Bouldering	Indian Dance	Skiing
Bowling	Jiu-Jitsu	Slackline
Boxing	Judo	Snowboarding
Breakdancing	Juggling	Snowshoeing
Capoeira	Karate	Soccer
ChiRunning	Kayaking	Softball
ChiWalking	Kickball	Surfing
Circus Arts	Kickboxing	Swinge Dance
Climbing Gym	Kiteboarding	Tabata
Cross-Country Skiing	Kung Fu	Tae Kwan Do
CrossFit	Mixed Martial Arts	Tough Mudder
Cuban Dance	Mountain Biking	Trampoline
Dance Classes	Mountain Climbing	Traveling Rings
Dodgeball	MovNat	Utlimate Frisbee
Dragon Boating	Paddleboarding	Warrior Dash
Folk Dance	Parkour	Wrestling
Frisbee	Pilates	Yoga
Geocaching	Pogo Stick	Zumba

Fitting Exercise into Your Schedule

All day long, you are doing your routine movement, ergonomics self-assessment, and posture improvement activities — at least I hope that you are, or at least trying to do them. Unlike those practices, exercise is typically an episodic activity. You can do it whenever it is convenient for you and your calendar. Given the hectic schedules that are typical in the lives of office workers like you, this is great news. Remember also that you can benefit from even the smallest amount of exercise, so anything you can work into your schedule will help.

Naturally, the more you do, the more you will benefit. So strive to meet or exceed the 30-minutes-five-times-a-week guidelines. But any amount of exercise is better than none. Even if you can fit in only a 10-minute run two or three times a week or a 5-minute "no-sweat workout" at your desk once or twice a day, you will get a bit more fit.

One common excuse offered to explain poor exercise habits is, "I'm just too busy." I am not going to call into question the actual busy-ness of your days. I will, however, point out that when most people objectively evaluate the actual use of their time, they usually find a lot more time available than they might have guessed. Stepping back every once in a while to take an impartial look at how you are spending your time — and recalling that you can benefit from exercise sessions of as little as ten minutes — may reveal more opportunities in your day for exercise.

This isn't a time-management book, though, so let's move on and get started on developing some exercise habits.

Developing Better Exercise Habits

Add a Tiny Habit

Recall B.J. Fogg's recipe for a Tiny Habit: After I [existing habit/anchor], I will [new tiny behavior]. Some ideas for Tiny Habits to jump-start your exercise habit:

- After I arrive at work, I will take 3 flights of stairs 2 or 3 steps at a time.
- After I walk to the copier, I will do 5 toe raises.
- As I wait at the printer, I will do 5 half squats.
- After I answer the phone, I will stand on one leg for 10 seconds.
- As I read an article online, I will supinate my forearms (rotate palms up) 5 times.
- After I read an article online, I will retract my head 5 times.
- After I write a long email, I will rotate my neck to each side 5 times.

147

- After I save a file, I will flex and extend my neck 5 times.
- As I wait for a meeting to start, I will do 5 sets of Kegel exercises.
- After I eat pour a cup of coffee, I will do 5 shallow lunges with each leg.
- After I eat lunch, I will take a 5-minute walk.
- After I finish my workday, I will call my workout partner to confirm our next exercise rendezvous.

Modify a Habit Loop

Recall Charles Duhigg's habit loop and how you can manipulate each part of it — the cue, the routine, and the reward — as well as the underlying craving. Here are some ideas to help you create, modify, or replace your exercise habit loops:

- Use classic cues to get started. If you don't currently have an exercise habit, one of the best ways to create one is to focus on the cues that will actually remind you to do your workouts. There is certainly no shortage of ideas for workout routines, and we all understand the basic rewards of regular exercise, so discovering and using cues is often the key to kicking off your new exercise habit. Two classic cues have helped millions of would-be exercisers get started. First is the time of day. If you put exercise in your calendar like any other obligation, and if you place it strategically in your day where it is least likely to be disrupted by other obligations, you'll have your best shot at establishing your exercise habit. The two best times of day for most people are either first thing in the morning or on the way home from work. The second classic cue is your gear. If you work out in the morning, laying out your exercise gear the night before (or even sleeping in it) will remind you that that's the first thing you're doing when you get up. If you work out after work, put your gym bag or other gear by your office door, on the front seat of your car, or in another place where you can't miss it.
- Mix up your routines. If you have an existing exercise habit, congratulations. But if you're one of the many people do the same exercise routine day after day, you're treading that fine line between having a routine and slipping into a rut, and you

may find yourself plateauing in your progress toward your fitness goals. If your current routines are keeping you on track, then by all means use that momentum to keep your exercise habit going. But altering your routines just a bit once in a while can keep your workouts fresh and interesting and make them more physically rewarding. So mix up your workouts once in a while. If you always use weight machines, try using free weights one day a week. If you always jog on the treadmill, try jogging outdoors one day a week. If you always do crunches for your core, try doing planks one day a week. The original fitness guru, Jack LaLanne, used to completely change his workout routine every month. You don't have to be that drastic, but any exercise regimen can benefit from regular variation.

- Consider the craving. Another way to mix up an exercise habit loop is to examine the underlying craving that drives it. If you currently do workouts that are designed to help you look good in a swimsuit, then a craving for a beach body may underlie your exercise habits. The cue for this kind of habit loop might be seeing your friends' flat stomachs and bulging biceps or viewing images of chiseled bodies in magazines, TV, and other media. Your current routine might consist mostly of exercises that tone and bulk up your pecs, biceps, and other classic beach muscles. Your reward is the ability to effortlessly slip into that swimsuit you wore in college. When you think back to the office-work body patterns described earlier in this chapter, though, you might notice that the push-ups, bench presses, biceps curls, and crunches common in beach-body workouts can also perpetuate and encourage those patterns. By adding some more deadlifts, squats, and trunk-extension exercises, you can still satisfy your craving for a buff body and address the patterns that your body is dealing with at work all day.
- Get creative with your rewards. We tend to focus on the intrinsic health and fitness rewards of exercise. When you look more closely at your exercise habit loops, though, you may find other rewards that can help keep you on track. A classic strategy for sticking with an exercise regimen is to have a workout partner. This works as a cue, of course, when your friend calls to remind you of your running date, but the

companionship of your friend on your run is in itself a reward. Many regular exercisers report clearer thinking and better work performance, so increased productivity is another reward of your exercise habit that you may have overlooked. Staying attuned to these kinds of tangential rewards of exercise can help you keep your habit loops tuned up.

Adopt a Practice

Finding practices to adopt is easier with exercise than in any other area. With tons of programs and systems to choose from, you shouldn't have any trouble finding enjoyable exercise systems that help keep you fit for work. Some ideas:

- If you are starting from scratch, programs like Couch to 5k — which prepares you to run a 5K race in 9 weeks — systematically guide you along a focused exercise path that can leave you with a new exercise habit.
- Calisthenics workouts use mostly bodyweight exercises like jumping jacks, push-ups, and lunges to do a quick full-body workout, often in a group setting. They were first developed by old-school exercise gurus like Jack LaLanne and remain popular to this day in many gyms and in programs like Al Kavadlo's Progressive Calisthenics.
- CrossFit mashes up exercises from high-intensity interval training, Olympic weightlifting, powerlifting, gymnastics, calisthenics, and strongman competitions into grueling workouts. CrossFit enthusiasts like the competitive, group setting for the workouts. It may not be the best choice if you're just getting started, but CrossFit can definitely get you in shape.
- MovNat and other "paleo" workouts, and parkour and similar playful workouts emphasize natural movements like pushing and pulling, running and jumping, hanging and swinging, crawling and climbing, and carrying and lifting.
- Rowing in sculls (two oars per person) or sweeps (one oar per person) is a fantastic remedy for desk posture. Its emphasis on leg power, trunk extension, and posterior-chain engagement is almost the exact opposite of what you do sitting in a chair all day. If you live somewhere cold or just don't feel like going

out in a boat, "ergs" — machines that mimic the actual rowing motion — are available in many gyms.

- If you dislike gyms or just prefer to work out at home, programs like the Insanity and P90X DVD programs show you how to do a vigorous workout at home. You can also easily put together your own workouts by browsing YouTube and other online video websites.

- Refer back to the "Fun Exercise Ideas" list a few pages ago. From aerial circus routines to Zumba dance, there's certainly a fun workout out there for you.

- Mind-body workouts like yoga, Pilates, and tai chi combine mindful concentration with physical activity. These classes come in as many styles, varieties, and intensity levels as there are teachers and studios, so you should be able to find a workout appropriate for your goals and fitness level.

Take a Plunge

Go nuts! Shake up your physical fitness life. Commit to a big exercise goal. Change careers. Here are just a few ideas to plunge into the world of exercise:

- Do a boot camp. Many personal trainers offer intense on-boarding programs that quickly get you into rigorous exercise routines.

- Commit to a competitive sport. Joining a volleyball or soccer team, registering for a series of tennis tournaments, or signing up as a member of a rowing team will require that you build your overall fitness, master the techniques of the event, and train for competition.

- Run a marathon or triathlon. Endurance events entail long training cycles that may very well leave you with a lifelong exercise habit.

- Climb a mountain. An expedition to a mountain peak requires both rigorous. Long-term physical preparation and commitment to logistics that are sure to engage you.

- Become a personal trainer. The fitness industry is a great place to make a living, and the perks include a work environment that encourages regular workouts and ready access to plenty of exercise gear.

Suggested Reading

The First 20 Minutes: Surprising Science Reveals How We Can: Exercise Better, Train Smarter, Live Longer, Gretchen Reynolds

FrameWork: Your 7-Step Program for Healthy Muscles, Bones, and Joints, Nicholas DiNubile and William Patrick

The American Physical Therapy Association Book of Body Maintenance and Repair, Marilyn Moffat

Strength Training Anatomy, Frederic Delavier

Sources

"2008 Physical Activity Guidelines for Americans." Health.gov (U.S. Office of Disease Prevention and Health Promotion). http://www.health.gov/

"Physical Activity for Everyone: The Benefits of Physical Activity." U.S. Centers for Disease Control and Prevention. http://www.cdc.gov/

"Training Principles to Improve Athlete Performance." Human-Kinetics, October 24, 2011. http://www.humankinetics.com/

Breene, Sophia. "13 Unexpected Benefits of Exercise." Greatist.com, October 7, 2013.

Delavier, Frederic, and Michael Gundill. Strength Training Anatomy Workout, The. 1 edition. Champaign, IL: Human Kinetics, 2011.

Delavier, Frederic. Strength Training Anatomy. 2 edition. Hershey, PA: Human Kinetics, 2005.

DiNubile, Nicholas A., and William Patrick. FrameWork: Your 7-Step Program for Healthy Muscles, Bones, and Joints. 1 edition. Rodale, 2005.

Duane, Daniel. "Fitness Crazed." The New York Times, May 24, 2014. http://www.nytimes.com/

Gibala, Martin J., Jonathan P. Little, Maureen J. MacDonald, and John A. Hawley. "Physiological Adaptations to Low-Volume, High-Intensity Interval Training in Health and Disease." The Journal of Physiology 590, no. 5 (March 1, 2012): 1077–84.

Hart, Lawrence. "Effect of Stretching on Sport Injury Risk: A Review." Clinical Journal of Sport Medicine: Official Journal of the Canadian Academy of Sport Medicine 15, no. 2 (March 2005): 113.

Jones, Matthew D., John Booth, Janet L. Taylor, and Benjamin K. Barry. "Aerobic Training Increases Pain Tolerance in Healthy Individuals." Medicine and Science in Sports and Exercise 46, no. 8 (August 2014): 1640–47.

Kendall, Florence Peterson. Muscles, Testing and Function: With Posture and Pain. 4th edition. Baltimore, Md: Lippincott Williams & Wilkins, 1993.

Kreider, Tim. "The 'Busy' Trap." NY Times "Opinionator" blog. http://opinionator.blogs.nytimes.com/

Lawrence, Jean. "Exercise at Your Desk." WebMD. http://www.webmd.com/

Lee, Duck-Chul, Russell R. Pate, Carl J. Lavie, Xuemei Sui, Timothy S. Church, and Steven N. Blair. "Leisure-Time Running Reduces All-Cause and Cardiovascular Mortality Risk." Journal of the American College of Cardiology 64, no. 5 (August 5, 2014): 472–81.

Mattes, Aaron L. Active Isolated Stretching: The Mattes Method. Sarasota, FL.: Aaron Mattes Therapy, 2000.

Medina, John. "Exercise" chapter in Brain Rules: 12 Principles for Surviving and Thriving at Work, Home, and School. Seattle, WA: Pear Press, 2008.

Merz, Theo. "Can 20 Seconds of High Intensity Exercise Really Beat a Session in the Gym?," January 22, 2014. http://www.telegraph.co.uk/

Micheo, William, Luis Baerga, and Gerardo Miranda. "Basic Principles Regarding Strength, Flexibility, and Stability Exercises." PM&R, Exercise and Sports for Health Promotion, Disease, and Disability, 4, no. 11 (November 2012): 805–11.

Milam, Emily. "Deskercise! 33 Smart Ways to Exercise at Work." Greatist, May 28, 2014. http://greatist.com/

Moffat, Marilyn. The American Physical Therapy Association Book of Body Maintenance and Repair. 1 edition. New York: Holt Paperbacks, 1999.

O'Sullivan, Kieran, Sean McAuliffe, and Neasa DeBurca. "The Effects of Eccentric Training on Lower Limb Flexibility: A Systematic Review." British Journal of Sports Medicine 46, no. 12 (September 1, 2012): 838–45.

Quinn, Elizabeth. "What Are the Exercise Principles of Conditioning?" About.com Sports Medicine. http://sportsmedicine.about.com/

Reynolds, Gretchen. The First 20 Minutes: Surprising Science Reveals How We Can: Exercise Better, Train Smarter, Live Longer. 1 edition. New York: Hudson Street Press, 2012.

Reynolds, Gretchen. The First 20 Minutes: Surprising Science Reveals How We Can: Exercise Better, Train Smarter, Live Longer. New York: Hudson Street Press, 2012.

Shrier, I. "Stretching before Exercise Does Not Reduce the Risk of Local Muscle Injury: A Critical Review of the Clinical and Basic Science Literature." Clinical Journal of Sport Medicine: Official Journal of the Canadian Academy of Sport Medicine 9, no. 4 (October 1999): 221–27.

Stone, Robert J. Atlas of Skeletal Muscles. 2nd edition. Dubuque, IA: William C Brown Pub, 1996.

Walker, Brad. The Anatomy of Stretching. Chichester, England: North Atlantic Books, 2007.

This is a partial list of sources consulted as I wrote this chapter, including only items mentioned or referred to above. For a full list of everything I read as I prepared this chapter, please visit sitless.com/chapter6

Acknowledgements

I am grateful for the generous assistance of many knowledgeable and supportive friends and colleagues.

Joan Vernikos, Former NASA Director of Life Sciences, was an enthusiastic and inspirational early interviewee, and I was delighted when she agreed to write the foreword for the book. Kristin Swanson at Northwestern University and Ravensara Travillian at the University of Washington have been superb guides as I have navigated the world of scientific research. I am grateful also for the many scientists working in the areas of sedentary studies, inactivity physiology, workplace ergonomics, exercise physiology, and other disciplines whose work provides the evidence-based foundation for *Scared Sitless*.

Many thanks to the friends who took the time to review and comment on the book at various stages in its development - Adelka Shawn, Becky Baker, Bonnie Bhatti, Caryl Fikse, Curt Rosengren, Daniel Pope, David Amdal, Heidi Swillinger, Joe Follansbee, Nancy Erickson, Peter Herford, Richard Bartlett, and Tim Koffley - and my apologies to anyone whose contributions I have overlooked.

My massage clients originally inspired me to write the book and have been an ongoing source of inspiration and a perceptive sounding board as I have developed it.

Many thanks to the organizers of events at which I have spoken or presented, among them Ignite Seattle, Seattle Maker Faire, Seattle WordPress Meetup, Washington State Podiatric Medical Assistants Association, American Society for Indexing, and Spark Weekend Seattle. Thanks also to my on-site consulting clients. I'd also like to give a big shout-out to my Toastmasters group, the Tough Tech Toasties in downtown Seattle.

While I have done most of the actual writing of this book at home, the Impact Hub Seattle co-working space has frequently served as my base of operations. I truly appreciate the community that Brian Howe and Lindsey Engh have created there – and the sit-stand workstations they provide. I have developed and honed many of the ideas in this book in conversation with Hub members, staff, mentors, and guests, among them Brad Struss, Candace Faber, Eldan Goldenberg, Fisher Qua, Gregory Heller, Kimo Jordan, Sean O'Connor, Shaula Massena, and Zachary Cohn.

Jane Ganter edited the book, and Richard Swanson proofread it. Charlotte Pierce of the Independent Publishers of New England has been supportive and generous as I have returned to the world of book publishing.

Any errors or oversights here are mine alone.

Made in the USA
Coppell, TX
19 May 2020

25759156R00104